TRUSTING GOD'S TIMING

What people are saying about *Trusting God's Timing*

The failure to fully comprehend what season of time we're currently in is a major factor in the confusion and frustration often associated with entering into the fullness of God's plan for our lives. Since we live in a highly technological age that promotes simple and easy access to almost anything desired, the idea of waiting on God is becoming increasingly difficult for people to understand. The ensuing result is that people who bypass the process unknowingly sabotage their destiny. Steven, by virtue of the wisdom gained through his own real-time experiences, has written this wonderful book to help us understand the concept of time and the dynamics thereof as connected to the call of God in life. *Trusting God's Timing* should be read by all believers, whether called to full-time ministry or not. It offers a plethora of information based on the lives of Joseph, David, and a host of others to help us avoid and overcome any pitfalls waiting to ensnare us along the way. He has masterfully shared his revelations about dealing with the process of time from the original call of God to its completion. I encourage you to read, meditate, and apply these truths to your life, and as you do, you will overcome the temptation to take the path of least resistance to the intended goal, and thus finish in the right time and the right place, as God originally intended.

—Pastor Brent Rudoski
Senior Pastor of Faith Alive Family Church, Saskatoon
Author, *Jesus Was Not a Rebel*

I have been a pastor for nearly twenty-five years. During that time I have met many people who have a dream from God. Many never see it fulfilled. They become frustrated with passing time, not realizing that Jesus is using that time to prepare them for their future. Steven's book gives great insight into the things God wants to accomplish in us during that time. We hear a lot about seed and harvest. But the Bible talks about seed, time, and harvest. This book will encourage all of us with the seed of a vision from God to enjoy the journey of passing time before entering into the harvest. A delay of the dream is not a denial. Allow this book to show you how God is using this time to get you ready for bigger things!

—Pastor Eric Johns
Senior Pastor of Buffalo Dream Center

God's Word is filled with promises for us to pursue and possess. Many believers today have received prophetic words and have visions from God. Unfortunately, all too often many believers become impatient or they give up on the promise in the season of waiting. Steven Stoffelsen has written an excellent book filled with insight and immediate help for believers who are learning to persist in pursuing the promises of God to completion. If you are waiting on the Lord, I know you will be encouraged and strengthened by this book.

—Pastor Matt Tapley
Lead Pastor, Lakemount Worship Centre

Many years ago I heard a prophet deliver a message to a man: "Preparation is not lost time." Over the years I have observed many abort or abandon the plan God has for their lives because they refuse to embrace the season of preparation. Character development is essential to longevity in ministry. Steven does a great job communicating these truths in his easy to read yet powerful insight into the concept of time and how the Father uses it. This book will encourage anyone who is weary with the process to enjoy the journey and stand firm in the midst of the struggle.

—Rev. Richard Ciaramitaro
President of Open Bible Faith Fellowship of Canada

Trusting God's Timing is a great word for many ministers to follow and adhere to. It is easy to read and absorb. The message in this book is a must for anyone with a vision and call from God to apply to their lives and ministry. I like the way Steven includes his own life story and challenges over the years. He shares from real experiences.

I have seen Steven grow from a shy young man who was afraid to talk to anyone to a bold, compassionate man of God walking in God's vision for his life. My story is much the same. I congratulate him for going way beyond his comfort zone and outside of what others have told him wasn't possible and walked by faith for the glory of God and His Kingdom.

—Kim Weiler
Founder of Fe Viva World Missions

TRUSTING GOD'S TIMING

*Standing in Faith
While You Wait*

Steven
STOFFELSEN

TRUSTING GOD'S TIMING
Copyright © 2017 by Steven Stoffelsen

All rights reserved. Neither this publication nor any part of this publication may be reproduced or transmitted in any form or by any means, electronic or mechanical, including photocopying, recording or any information storage and retrieval system, without permission in writing from the author.

Unless otherwise indicated, all scripture quotations taken from the New American Standard Bible® (NASB), Copyright © 1960, 1962, 1963, 1968, 1971, 1972, 1973, 1975, 1977, 1995 by The Lockman Foundation. Used by permission. www.Lockman.org. Scripture quotations marked (NIV) are taken from the Holy Bible, New International Version®, NIV®. Copyright © 1973, 1978, 1984, 2011 by Biblica, Inc.™ Used by permission of Zondervan. All rights reserved worldwide. www.zondervan.com The "NIV" and "New International Version" are trademarks registered in the United States Patent and Trademark Office by Biblica, Inc.™ Scripture quotations marked (NKJV) taken from the New King James Version®. Copyright © 1982 by Thomas Nelson. Used by permission. All rights reserved. Scripture quotations marked (KJV) taken from the Holy Bible, King James Version, which is in the public domain.

ISBN: 978-1-4866-1400-4 Printed in Canada

Word Alive Press
131 Cordite Road, Winnipeg, MB R3W 1S1
www.wordalivepress.ca

Library and Archives Canada Cataloguing in Publication

Stoffelsen, Steven, author
    Trusting God's timing : standing in faith while you wait / Steven Stoffelsen.

Issued in print and electronic formats.
ISBN 978-1-4866-1400-4 (softcover).--ISBN 978-1-4866-1401-1 (ebook)

    1. Expectation (Psychology)--Religious aspects--Christianity.
2. Patience--Religious aspects--Christianity. 3. Trust in God--Christianity. I. Title.

BV4647.E93S76 2017   248.4   C2017-900196-5
                                         C2017-900197-3

I dedicate this book to my amazing wife, Karla, who has been a great inspiration to me. Thank you for helping me through the tough times when it was hard to see that the promise would finally be fulfilled.

CONTENTS

	Acknowledgements	xiii
	Foreword	xv
	Introduction	xix
1.	Faithfulness: Your Launchpad to Success	1
2.	Stand the Test of Time	13
3.	Hardships Come to Make Us Stronger	27
4.	Called to Greatness Yet Willing to Serve	47
5.	The Importance of Friendships	63
6.	Seeking God: The Key to Success	71
7.	God's Way, Not Your Way	79
8.	Wait for God's Direction	91
	Conclusion	97

ACKNOWLEDGEMENTS

First of all, I would like to acknowledge my Lord and Saviour Jesus Christ, who has taught me—and continues to teach me—every lesson in this book. It has been a long, wonderful journey, and I can't wait for what's ahead.

I want to thank my mother, Janet Stoffelsen, who first looked over the manuscript and believed in me from the beginning.

Deborah Grady, thank you for being the first person to attempt to professionally edit my rough manuscript. I know that it wasn't an easy job. You did awesome. I would recommend you to everybody.

Thanks to Adam Biro for your friendship and advice throughout the book. You helped to make it a success.

Thanks to all the mentors God has placed in my life. You know who you are. Pastor Brent Rudoski, thank you for encouraging me at a time when I was ready to give up, even though you didn't know it. Your words made an impact on my life.

Thanks also to Word Alive Press. Your advice and expertise have helped me enormously. Your contest was what made all this possible. Thanks for making my dream of becoming a writer a reality.

FOREWORD

A few years ago, I passed through the tiny community of Between, Georgia. With a population of only 148, the place isn't much to write home about. The name fits because it's halfway between Atlanta and Athens. But as I drove through, I couldn't help imagining the strange reactions I'd get if I lived there.

"Where are you from?" someone would ask.

"I live in Between."

"In between what?"

"In Between, Georgia."

"In between Georgia and what?"

I doubt I'll ever move to that town, but the truth is that many of us are living "in between" because we're in a major transition. Some of us know where we're going, but we feel stuck halfway. Or we may sense God is moving us into a new spiritual assignment, yet the process of getting there is inching forward about as fast as a Siberian glacier.

If you're moving at that pace, and are frustrated with the fact that God's promises are slow in coming, then this book is for you.

I struggle with all the emotions that accompany a major transition. I've battled doubts ("Did God really promise this?"), fears ("What if He doesn't provide?"), confusion ("Last week I was sure; this week I'm not so sure") and impatience ("Lord, I need some answers *now!*").

But I've discovered some things we can do to make the transition smoother.

First, we must let go of the past. Sometimes we end up in spiritual limbo because we hold on to memories, relationships, and that which is secure and comfortable. When Naomi felt called to return to Bethlehem, her daughter-in-law Orpah refused to go because she preferred what was culturally familiar. We must leave nostalgia behind.

Second, we must let go of our doubts. It's easy to fall into the trap of double-mindedness. We say we want to go to our promised land, but we drag our feet. We say we want to go forward, but we're like a moving car that has its parking brake engaged. Faith requires you to release the brake! James warns the double-minded person: *"For that man ought not to expect that he will receive anything from the Lord"* (James 1:7). Doubt will stop you from shifting forward.

Third, we must welcome those whom God sends to help you. The body of Christ has many members, and those who are gifted as prophets, intercessors, counsellors, and encouragers will always show up when you're in strategic moments of transition. When Moses was weary of the battle and could barely find the strength to pray, God sent Aaron and Hur to lift up his arms (Exodus 17:12). When Mary was perplexed by the daunting task of carrying the Messiah in her womb, Elizabeth released a prophetic blessing over her (Luke 1:41–45).

Don't go through transition alone. Ask your friends to pray with you. They are the spiritual midwives who will help you birth God's promise when you don't have the strength to deliver.

Fourth, you must fight for your promise. The devil is a thief, and he doesn't want us to receive God's promises or advance into new spiritual territory. This is why you must wield

Foreword

God's promise as a weapon. Paul told Timothy to fight the good fight *"in accordance with the prophecies previously made concerning you"* (1 Timothy 1:18). Declare God's prophetic promises over your life. His Word will break satanic resistance.

This book by my friend Steven Stoffelsen emphasizes the fact that God's promises are rarely fulfilled overnight. If you have a promise from God, you must wait. Faith is a journey, and it has a starting point and a final destination. But it also has a "between," and many of us struggle the most when we're in that stage of waiting. Steven has waited a long time to see his promises fulfilled, but during the waiting stage he discovered some valuable truths that will help you stay close to your Shepherd, Jesus Christ, during the long expedition.

God knows your ultimate destination. He is committed to guiding you, even when you walk through the valley of the shadow of death to get there. He will not leave you in the land of Between. With His rod and staff, He will usher you into your promised territory.

—Lee Grady
Former editor of *Charisma* magazine
Director of The Mordecai Project
(an international missions organization)

INTRODUCTION

We all want to see God move in our lives to accomplish His will—or it should be the desire of everyone who claims to be a Christian. God created you for a purpose. Once you know what that purpose is, you won't be satisfied until it is fulfilled.

I believe that you have picked up this book so you could be encouraged to follow the call of God on your life with perseverance. Whether you're a new believer or a seasoned one, God wants to complete the work He has begun in you.

This book is for those who want to run with the vision God has given them. My desire is to see you fulfill the call God has placed on your life. Don't push to make your own will come true, but follow the path God has for you. As you stand firm and submit to His calling, even in difficult times, God will accomplish His purpose in your life.

In this book, we're going to look at the importance of time. We'll see how, when circumstances seem hardest, that's when we're about to see God move on our behalf. It's not time to give up; it's time to run with the vision God has given you. Learn from your mistakes and mishaps and grow in God. Difficulties often come so our character may develop and strengthen. God's more concerned about you growing in Him than He is about your calling. Your calling will come to pass, but God wants you to be like Him. He wants you to be all you were called to be.

Have you ever looked closely at the story of Jairus when he thought he was about to lose his daughter? He was desperate for her healing, and the only one who could help him was Jesus. He knew he had to run to Him and ask for help, but he had seen how hard it could be to get through the crowds and encounter Jesus. Time was running out and this was his only chance. He was frantic for the life of his daughter.

When he found Jesus, Jairus asked Him to come to his home to heal his daughter. Jesus agreed and began to walk with Jairus toward the house. While walking, Jairus was most likely frightened, sure that time was running out and his daughter would die if they arrived too late. But if they got there on time, Jesus would heal her. Jairus was doing his best to expect a miracle, but he was tormented with doubt. He'd heard many stories of the miracles and healings Jesus had done. He had most likely seen people receive their sight and the lame walk. Now tragedy had hit his home and he had to see that miracles could happen for him just as it had for others. He needed to experience personally what Jesus would do for him.

Luke, being a doctor, goes into a bit more depth in his version of the story. It's very important to see that the miracles of Jesus aren't just for others; they're for you. What Jesus will do for one, He will do for another, for He is *"no respecter of persons"* (Acts 10:34, KJV).

> *And there came a man named Jairus, and he was an official of the synagogue; and he fell at Jesus' feet, and began to implore Him to come to his house; for he had an only daughter, about twelve years old, and she was dying. But as He went, the crowds were pressing against Him.*
>
> —Luke 8:41–42

Introduction

Can you imagine the urgency Jairus felt? The panic? Luke writes that Jairus fell at Jesus' feet and began to implore Him. Jairus saw the crowds, but he felt that his situation was more important than anyone else's. There wasn't any higher priority at that moment than his daughter. The crowds could wait; he needed his miracle right away.

The Gospel of Matthew shows us that Jesus began to follow him: *"Jesus got up and began to follow him, and so did His disciples"* (Matthew 9:19). I'm sure Jairus was excited. Jesus was following him; He felt compassion for Jairus' situation. I bet Jairus wanted to run so they could get there faster. Hope rose in his heart! Jesus, the one who had come to heal the sick, was coming to his house to heal his dying daughter. Nothing was going to stop Jairus from receiving his miracle.

Then, just when his fear and panic subsided, they encountered a dreaded delay.

> *And a woman who had a hemorrhage for twelve years, and could not be healed by anyone, came up behind Him and touched the fringe of His cloak, and immediately her hemorrhage stopped. And Jesus said, "Who is the one who touched Me?"*
>
> *And while they were all denying it, Peter said, "Master, the people are crowding and pressing in on You."*
>
> *But Jesus said, "Someone did touch Me, for I was aware that power had gone out of Me."*
>
> —Luke 8:43–46

Jairus was impatient. Jesus had to get to his daughter, yet He stopped to ask who had touched Him. How could Jesus be so insensitive to his needs? Jairus may not have understood what was happening, but Jesus did. Jesus knew He had everything under control and that there was time to take notice of this woman and heal her and everything would still be okay with Jairus' daughter.

Put yourself in Jairus' shoes. If your little girl was dying and Jesus was on His way to help, would you have faith even during the delay?

Jairus had to put his feelings aside. He had to continue to trust that his miracle had been provided for. Jesus wasn't just going to leave him there. Jesus wasn't going to start walking towards his house and then decide along the way that He wasn't going to go. What Jesus starts, He will surely finish.

It may take some time, but Jesus knows what He's doing. He may need to bless someone else first, but your blessing has already been paid for. Hang in there.

> *When the woman saw that she had not escaped notice, she came trembling and fell down before Him, and declared in the presence of all the people the reason why she had touched Him, and how she had been immediately healed. And He said to her, "Daughter, your faith has made you well; go in peace."*
>
> —Luke 8:47–48

We aren't sure how this lady even got close to Jesus. According to the law, she wasn't allowed to walk among the people. She was an outcast with an emission of blood, as was written about in the Old Testament (Leviticus 15:26–27). Anything she touched would be declared unclean. She was marked by society so no one could come near her, or even touch anything she touched. She had suffered this way for twelve years, since the time Jairus' daughter had been born.

How could this outcast think she could receive her healing before the synagogue official did? How could she dare come near Him in her uncleanliness? The answer is that there was something different about Jesus. Everyone else judged, but Jesus always showed mercy to those who touched Him. Prostitutes and thieves could come near to Jesus without being turned away. This brought faith to the woman. If anyone could do anything for her, it was Jesus.

Jesus stopped right in the middle of what He was doing, showing everyone that this woman was important to Him despite her status. He would touch anyone who had faith in Him. It didn't matter if you were of the highest or lowest rank, Jesus was ready to heal. This is why Jesus could stop and make Jairus, a synagogue official, wait a while longer.

Randy Clark, in his book *Power to Heal*, put it this way:

> *She approached Jesus with disregard for her religious tradition that required her to stay out of public—especially away from holy people. That is "if I can" faith in action and it is often spelled r-i-s-k. She took a tremendous risk, including the possibility of stoning, when she approached Jesus. People who have very weak faith or some faith will not take extreme risks like this… If any person had the reason to give up on the possibility of being healed, it was this woman. However, she still had faith to receive her healing after twelve years.*[1]

Before hearing about all the miracles Jesus had performed, this woman had given up hope. The doctors and the medicines they prescribed had repeatedly let her down, but when she heard about Jesus, faith began to arise inside her. She easily could have given up before she received her healing.

---

1 Randy Clark, *Power to Heal* (Shippensburg, PA: Destiny Image, 2015), 237–238.

Once the procession ground to a halt, the very news Jairus had feared came to him: his daughter had died. Jesus could no longer do anything for him—or could He? Let's go back to the Scriptures:

> *While He was still speaking, someone came from the house of the synagogue official, saying, "Your daughter has died; do not trouble the Teacher anymore." But when Jesus heard this, He answered him, "Do not be afraid any longer; only believe, and she will be made well."*
>
> —Luke 8:49–50

Jairus' hope evaporated. He wasn't going to see the miracle he had been waiting for. It was too late. If only he had made it there sooner, or if Jesus hadn't stopped, this wouldn't have happened. So many thoughts must gone through his head when he heard the bad news.

A lot of people would give up at this point. They wouldn't wait to hear what Jesus said next. They hear negative news and shut down. They see that Jesus has blessed someone else and figure He'll do it for others, but not for them. But if we would only wait a bit longer, we would see our miracle. Don't give up at the first sign of bad news. Continue trusting in Jesus, because He came to save and deliver.

> *When He came to the house, He did not allow anyone to enter with Him, except Peter and John and James, and the girl's father and mother. Now they were all weeping and lamenting for her; but He said, "Stop weeping, for she has not died, but is asleep." And they began laughing at Him, knowing that she had died. He, however, took her by the hand and called, saying, "Child, arise!" And her spirit returned, and she got up immediately; and He gave orders for*

Introduction

something to be given her to eat. Her parents were amazed;
but He instructed them to tell no one what had happened.
—Luke 8:51–56

Thankfully, Jairus decided not to give up. He had to wait, but God's timing is always perfect. He's never early and He's never late. He's always right on time. Jairus held on, even though it looked like this woman had been healed at the expense of his little girl. He chose to take Jesus at His Word and wait to see his miracle.

So often in our Christian walk, time kills us. We think that the vision God has given us is for right now. When it takes longer than expected, we're too quick to give up. Too often we've already readied Plan B in case what God showed us doesn't work out. God doesn't want us to have a Plan B. If we have a Plan B, it's because we don't believe God's plan with our whole hearts.

At this point in your life, you may be thinking, *Will God's plan for my life ever come true? It's sure taking a long time. Did I miss it?* I want to reassure you that if you're walking in obedience, you're right on track. It may take longer than you expected, but God's timing is always perfect. Trust in Him and you'll see God's promises fulfilled.

Life can often be a struggle. When hope seems lost, God calls us to rise up in faith. Know that God will do what He promised. Throughout the Bible, we see how God came through for His people. God doesn't change. He's always the same, always faithful. What He did in the lives of those recorded in the Bible, He will do for you today. He kept His promises then, and rest assured He will keep His promises today.

Trials and tests are a part of life. I'm not going to tell you that they'll never happen to you—because they will. If you're going through a storm in your life right now, faith will help you see beyond the storm. Faith is the key in every area of our lives, for *"without faith it is impossible to please God, because anyone who comes to him must believe that he exists and that he rewards those who earnestly seek him"* (Hebrews 11:6, NIV).

As we move ahead in our journey to see the fulfillment of God's call on our lives, we need faith. It's the only way. We can't do it on our own or control the way it unfolds; faith requires us to fully depend on God. He wants to take you through a process to develop this faith. He wants what you do today to impact the generations to come. Remember, He called you to help build His kingdom on earth. Even though He uses you, it isn't about you! Through this process, you become the kind of person who brings Him glory.

Over the years, I've seen people give up because the trials became too difficult and they weren't ready or willing to allow God to work in their lives. Some didn't want to wait for God's preparation before stepping into their calling. They wanted to fulfill their vision before they were ready, so they went out on their own—without the character development. They expected that God would do things according to their own schedule.

God won't speed things up just because you're impatient. He won't put you in a place you're not ready for. He'll mould and shape you until you're prepared for His best. His desire is for you to succeed in life. This is why He won't allow your vision to be fulfilled until He's done His perfect work in you. This takes time. We usually don't like the process. We often don't want to wait or allow God to touch certain hidden areas of our lives.

If we push to make the vision God gave us come to pass, we're doomed to fail. We must allow God to work in us. The process could take years, even decades, but the time of preparation is never a waste. God knows what we need in order to succeed in His vision for our lives. Often, we think we're ready

Introduction

so we get impatient, but God doesn't. He will work with you until He knows you're ready for all He has for you.

The Bible gives us examples of people who tried to do things when they became impatient. God seemed to be taking too long, so they decided to do things their own way. It didn't go well for them. Don't let impatience destroy the call of God on your life.

King Saul was the king chosen by the people of Israel. At the beginning of his reign, all seemed to be going well. However, his impatience destroyed him. He was supposed to wait for Samuel to come and offer a burnt offering, because priests were the only ones allowed under God's law to perform the offering, but read what he did instead:

> *Saul remained at Gilgal, and all the troops with him were quaking with fear. He waited seven days, the time set by Samuel; but Samuel did not come to Gilgal, and Saul's men began to scatter. So he said, "Bring me the burnt offering and the fellowship offerings." And Saul offered up the burnt offering. Just as he finished making the offering, Samuel arrived, and Saul went out to greet him.*
> *"What have you done?" asked Samuel.*
> —1 Samuel 13:7–11, NIV

Saul just needed to wait a few more minutes. His outcome may have been different had he waited for God's timing. As soon as he finished sending up the offering, Samuel arrived. Saul's breakthrough was just a few minutes away, but he panicked, got impatient, and decided to do things his way. We must always wait for God, even when He seems to be late.

> *Saul replied, "When I saw that the men were scattering, and that you did not come at the set time, and that the*

> *Philistines were assembling at Mikmash, I thought, 'Now the Philistines will come down against me at Gilgal, and I have not sought the Lord's favor.' So I felt compelled to offer the burnt offering."*
>
> *"You have done a foolish thing," Samuel said. "You have not kept the command the Lord your God gave you; if you had, he would have established your kingdom over Israel for all time. But now your kingdom will not endure; the Lord has sought out a man after his own heart and appointed him ruler of his people, because you have not kept the Lord's command."*
>
> —1 Samuel 13:11–14, NIV

At first, Saul's excuse sounds really good—as if he wants to seek God's favour and make sure everything is okay between him and God. However, things weren't right and Samuel let him know it. Saul stepped out of his calling as king to do a priestly duty, revealing his lack of faith and honour towards God. And Samuel pronounced the consequence for this sin.

This truly is a sad story. God would have done great things through him. He would have had a legacy. But since he was impatient and rebelled against God's law, he lost everything. This is an admonition for us to do things God's way. When we do, He'll do great things through us that will last for generations.

I like what R.T. Kendall says about this story in his book *Holy Fire*.

> *King Saul later became "yesterday's man" because he did not respect the explicit command regarding who is qualified to offer the burnt offering (part of the ceremonial law). He was to wait for Samuel but didn't. "Bring me the burnt offering," Saul commanded. Someone should have stopped him or at*

Introduction

least cautioned him. No one did. He then offered the burnt offering. When Samuel arrived, Saul explained that he felt "compelled" to do this... Although he became "yesterday's man" in that moment, he wore the crown for another twenty years. Twenty years without God's favor, but the people had no idea of this only Samuel (1 Samuel 16:1).[2]

I don't know about you, but I never want to become "yesterday's man." I want to be a part of what God's doing today. We need God's favour upon our lives at all times. Let's not grow weary and impatient. Let's obey God at all costs.

Like Saul, many people give up right before their breakthrough comes. We're prone to throw in the towel when things get tough. It's time we start to see difficult circumstances as stepping stones into our callings. When things seem too hard, that's when we're about to see something great happen. We weren't called to give up halfway. We were called to go all the way with Jesus. God's plans for you never change. He's called you from the beginning and has put His gifts inside of you. His Word says that the *"gifts and the calling of God are irrevocable"* (Romans 11:29).

Get ready to be challenged as we look at different people in the Bible and how they continued believing God even though much time had passed and they had suffered much hardship. They knew God had called them, and that what He had promised He was able to perform (Romans 4:21).

I don't know how long you've waited in faith, but God says, "Hold on." He wants you to realize that He's still working on your character and getting you ready for what He's called you to do. There's a blessing in the waiting. There's joy in knowing that the vision will come to pass, even though it

---

2 R.T. Kendall, *Holy Fire* (Lake Mary, FL: Charisma House, 2014), 60.

was given long ago. Even if God gave you the vision while you were a little child, He has not given up. Decide to believe today! Dust off the vision, pick it up, and run with it. God's ready to show His power through you. May this book encourage you to *"[f]ight the good fight of faith"* (1 Timothy 6:12).

If it seems that everyone except you is being blessed, know that God wants to do it for you. God wants to bless you as much as He has blessed others. Keep holding on and know that the blessing is going to come. Hardships are temporary, but they won't change your outcome—as long as you don't let them.

FAITHFULNESS: YOUR LAUNCHPAD TO SUCCESS

chapter one

For the past fourteen years, I've been serving under the spiritual covering of Fe Viva World Missions. It has been an incredible fourteen years with lots of opportunities for growth. I first came to Guatemala as a young missionary wanting to preach the Gospel, change the world, and see the power of God manifested. I pray that would be every Christian's dream. I had no idea how to accomplish this, but I knew God had called me to the mission field, specifically to Guatemala.

I came with many aspirations and expecting God to do amazing things through my life. I began to serve anywhere I could. I preached in churches and prisons, on the streets and in buses. I led worship and helped with mission teams. There were many opportunities for me to serve. I found that as I served in these different areas, God prepared me for my calling. As I walked the streets, I saw the homeless and forgotten. I would be on my way to church and have to pass through the red-light district. It pulled my heartstrings every time.

I used to walk the streets of Chiquimulilla, praying and asking God how I could make an impact. I asked God why He had called me to such a place. I was serving under another man's ministry and knew I should continue to do just that. There was more in store, but for the time I was doing the right thing.

Trusting God's Timing

Over time, I felt called to the red-light district, where there was lots of work to do. Most people had become calloused to those people, but all I felt was love and compassion for them. Many times I saw how people avoided any interaction with the homeless, either by walking around them or taking a giant step over them. This broke my heart, as I knew God wanted someone to care for these people.

One day, my leader, Kim Weiler, came to me and asked how I was feeling and where I felt God was leading me. He knew I was serving in many areas, but he wanted to know where God was calling me specifically. Once I told him, he said I should continue to seek God for more specifics on how I could serve the street people.

I took his advice and began to seek the Lord. I'll never forget the day we visited a church and Kim spoke. He said that he saw angels in the church. He called people to the altar and many wept there before the Lord. God touched my life that day in a way that marked me forever.

As I wept, Kim felt God giving people visions, and to some it was very specific. God was showing me things about the street people. He told me to bring them food, pray for them, and get to know them. He also gave me a mission statement: to love the unloved and reach the unreached.

Up to that point, I had made deals with God as to how long I would stay in Guatemala. The first time, I went for ten days. When God called me back, I told Him I would go for four months. During that time, I knew God was calling me to a longer commitment. Once again, I made a deal and said I would return for one year. However, at this service, where I received a powerful touch of God's presence, He said to me, "If you're going to take up this mantle, you can no longer give Me time limits. You must stay here until I say you can leave."

That Sunday morning changed the course of my life. I decided to pick up the mantle and reach out to the street people. Right away I let Kim know what had happened and what God had shown me. He was happy to hear it, and his words helped me start my ministry. He told me there was a need for that type of ministry, even though he personally had never felt called to it. He said he would help me with advice and pray for me, but that the ministry would be my baby. I would need to raise funds, share the vision, and run it myself. This gave me a sense of ownership, and I knew he believed I had what it took to lead a ministry.

But that didn't mean I worked alone. Another missionary was in Guatemala with us, and Kim suggested I talk to her about my idea. She had worked in a similar ministry in Philadelphia. It was then that I became good friends with the late Carol Gleeson, who showed me the ropes. We would go to the city's central park, where we knew people would approach us and ask for money. Instead of giving them money, we brought packed lunches and asked if they were hungry. They answered yes every time. We then sat down with them as they ate and asked questions about their families. We found that they often did have families, but their addictions to drugs and alcohol had been too much to handle, so they now lived alone on the streets.

We also worked with a local church for two years, hosting lunches and sharing the Gospel with the street men every Sunday. Do you know how many people I saw give their lives to Jesus? Not one. I served two years without seeing any fruit. I was ready to throw in the towel, but I knew God had called me and I had to be faithful, even though I wasn't seeing results.

The church we were working with no longer agreed with what we were doing because there had been no fruit. They thought the best thing to do was stop the feeding program and start working with children. I knew in my heart there was more, but the doors had closed.

I continued to visit the men on the street. I stuck with it even though others didn't believe in what I was doing. I'm sure some thought it would have been best for me to stop at that point. After all, everyone else had rejected the ministry. What more could I do?

I felt led to rent a house and make the ministry a full-time outreach to men. We opened the House of Refuge in February 2005. In March, we received the first occupant, twenty-five-year-old Edgar. He was sick and had no family in the area, as they'd moved away without telling him. In one night, he was saved, healed, and delivered and began living for Jesus. After two years of ministry, once the house opened we had our first convert within a month. God was showing me that He was faithful and would bring the fruit.

We have seen many people saved since Edgar, and the ministry keeps expanding. Once I married Karla, she began reaching out to women in prostitution and the sex trade. We have a breakfast for them once a month to share the love of Jesus. God shows up every time!

When it comes to seeing God's vision come to pass in our lives, we need to look at an important prerequisite. God won't place you into your destiny until you've learned to live a life of faithful service and submission. Don't expect God to bring you to the next level until you've developed experience. Anyone who doesn't learn how to submit and be faithful under leadership will never walk in the fullness of his or her calling. If you've never been faithful or submitted to someone else, how can you expect others to be faithful and submissive to you?

Ministry means teamwork. Cooperative support is necessary to get the work of the kingdom done. These truths are hard for many people to hear and obey. Everyone is tempted to do things their own way and think they can do things better than everyone else.

It's so important to catch this. If you don't, it'll take you a lot longer to see your vision fulfilled. Try to skip this step and you'll run into lots of heartache and discouragement. It truly isn't worth it.

So many people want a title, for example, thinking that's what will bring them importance. A title doesn't give us importance. Our value and sense of importance is rooted in the fact that God loves us and sent His Son to die for us. We are special in His sight. Besides, the only title we'll keep when we get to heaven is that of a servant. Look at what Jesus tells us about this:

His lord said to him, "Well done, good and faithful servant; you have been faithful over a few things, I will make you ruler over many things. Enter into the joy of your lord."
—Matthew 25:23, NKJV

This verse clearly says that the servant in question is being made a ruler over many things, yet his lord starts off by calling him a good and faithful servant. A good way to look at this is to recognize that the only title you'll have in the end is that of a servant. When you get to heaven, God isn't going to call you a good and faithful apostle, evangelist, or prophet. God will call you His servant. Your title means nothing at the end of time. Whatever you are in this life, you'll be called a servant in eternity.

Stop wasting time making apostleship your aim. Don't spend all your strength becoming the next great evangelist. Focus on serving Jesus by serving His people; allow Him to place you where He wants you. Make knowing Jesus your highest aim, not achieving a title, for the latter produces pride and stunts growth. If you want to see the vision God gave you fulfilled, you must seek Him as a servant.

As we make serving Jesus our top priority, we'll find where we can serve Him best. Jesus taught us to be under authority. You need to find a church and serve your pastor. Don't think you can be in a position of authority without serving a local church. There are too many lone rangers in the world today. If we haven't been under authority, we can't expect people to follow our authority.

Jesus said, *"And if you have not been faithful in what is another man's, who will give you what is your own?"* (Luke 16:12, NKJV) You might ask, isn't that verse speaking about finances? If you look at the full context (which you should), you'll find that, yes, it's mainly speaking about finances. However, Jesus from the start of the chapter is teaching about stewardship and serving others.

As you faithfully serve, without looking for credit, God will prepare you for leadership so others can serve under you. This is the order God has set up. We shouldn't try to sidestep God's established order.

Our ministry in Guatemala continues to expand to this day. Soon we plan to build the City of Refuge, which will be a place where men can come to recover and learn a trade at the same time. It'll be a training ground where men can become useful to society once again.

What would have happened if, after two years of not seeing any fruit, I had given up? If I hadn't been faithful in the discouraging times, I wouldn't have seen people get saved and healed. You need to be faithful. If you know God has called you to something specific, continue with it. You shouldn't give up at the first sign of disappointment. Stick it out. Our ministry wouldn't have been able to grow had I not been faithful.

Faithfulness: Your Launchpad to Success

I've continued to serve at Fe Viva in Guatemala, with House of Refuge a branch of that ministry. Recently, Kim asked us to take the next step and establish our own identity in Guatemala. It's time for us to grow on our own. Not because of struggling or strife, but because the ministry has grown successful.

This is healthy growth. Many ministries split because they aren't in agreement or because one thinks they can do better than the other. This is a terrible state to be in. Most of these ministries never grow because they have a root of rebellion. This is why having faithfulness in others will bring you much success. You can learn so much from serving others, things that will prepare you for leadership. If you want to lead, you must first learn the art of servanthood. That's what biblical leadership is all about: serving!

Think of the people in the Bible who first served someone else before becoming leaders. Some even served under ungodly leadership, but due to their faithfulness they were launched into success. Joseph served Pharaoh and the prison master before he was ready to be a leader. Joshua served under Moses' ministry for many years before succeeding Moses after he died.

Ruth first decided to leave her gods and serve her mother-in-law, Naomi. Nothing seemed to be going well for her after her husband died, but because she was faithful and made that declaration of faith, she said to Naomi,

> *For wherever you go, I will go; and wherever you lodge, I will lodge; Your people shall be my people, and your God, my God.*
> —Ruth 1:16, NKJV

She was able to meet and marry Boaz and then became the great-grandmother of King David, who was in the messianic lineage of Jesus. She received this honour because she decided to cling to her mother in law (Ruth 1:14).

Even though Saul tried to kill David, he remained faithful. David served Saul even in difficult times when others told him he was crazy for not killing the king. David learned to be faithful, knowing that God always has the final say and would protect him. Since he had been anointed to be king, nothing could prevent him from sitting on the throne.

Elisha also learned the importance of serving under another man's ministry. The prophet Elijah not only foretold the future but also performed many powerful miracles. He was God's man of the hour. Elisha knew it was important to serve under him. He was so faithful to him that he didn't want him to go on his own (2 Kings 2:3–6). Elisha was faithful right to the end.

Once Elijah left him, Elisha wanted to see the same miracles. He wanted to continue the work and be used of God in the same way. The first thing he did when Elijah was taken up into heaven was cry out to God: *"Where is the Lord God of Elijah?"* (2 Kings 2:14, NKJV) He was hungry for a move of God. Since he was faithful, he saw powerful miracles in his own ministry.

Of course, I have to mention the disciples who first learned to serve under Jesus. All of them, except Judas Iscariot, became powerful servants of Jesus. Why? It's simple: they were faithful under Jesus' ministry.

What about Jesus? Jesus was the most faithful of all. He was faithful to God Himself, even though so many rejected Him. He went against the stream but stayed obedient to His Father.

> *...though He was a Son, yet He learned obedience by the things which He suffered.*
> —Hebrews 5:8, NKJV

He was in no way a rebel. For more on this subject, I suggest you read my friend Pastor Brent Rudoski's book, *Jesus Was Not a Rebel*.[3]

If you want to be a leader and believe that God has called you into ministry, be faithful under someone else, even if you aren't one hundred percent in agreement with them. You may even need to serve in an area different from the one you feel called to. That's fine. Be faithful and diligent. God will raise you up in His perfect timing. If you haven't had the experience of working under others, your ministry will take longer to launch—and it will be hard. Prepare yourself by getting a mentor. Learn what it takes to be a leader from someone who already is one.

Let's look at some powerful words about submitting to godly leadership:

> *Obey those who rule over you, and be submissive, for they watch out for your souls, as those who must give account. Let them do so with joy and not with grief, for that would be unprofitable for you.*
>
> —Hebrews 13:17, NKJV

It is profitable for you to obey other leaders as they lead you in godly ways. You may be a leader of your own soon enough, but it's important to be accountable to someone. We should all have leaders over us who can speak into our lives and correct us if we go wrong. God designed it that way.

Another thing I should mention is this: if you're involved in gossip and backbiting against your leader, you're not in

---

[3] Brent Rudoski, *Jesus Was Not a Rebel* (Winnipeg, MB: Word Alive Press, 2014).

submission. You may appear to be by the way you do things, but your heart isn't right. You mustn't talk bad about your leaders.

When we talk about God's kind of faithfulness, it needs to be in all areas, not just the visible ones. It's easy to talk bad about our leaders and find faults with them, because not one is perfect. However, that doesn't give us a right to expose their faults.

If we're going to live faithfully the way God would have us live, we must uplift and pray for our leaders. If we tear them down, we're sowing bad seeds that we'll reap later. If you've been bad-talking your leader, repent now and choose to no longer participate in it.

O Lord, who may abide in Your tent? Who may dwell on Your holy hill? He who walks with integrity, and works righteousness, and speaks truth in his heart. He does not slander with his tongue, nor does evil to his neighbour...
—Psalm 15:1–3

Slandering our leaders will interfere with God's presence in our lives. If we want to see God's promise fulfilled in our lives, we must learn to bite our tongues and not speak evil of others, not just leaders.

Do you remember what happened to Miriam and Aaron when they began to murmur against their Moses? It was a very serious offense.

Then Miriam and Aaron spoke against Moses because of the Cushite woman whom he had married (for he had married a Cushite woman); and they said, "Has the Lord indeed spoken only through Moses? Has He not spoken through us as well?" And the Lord heard it.
—Numbers 12:1–2

Here Miriam and Aaron saw a fault in Moses. They began to expose how he had married a Cushite woman, a non-Israelite. They began to speak as though God would speak through them rather than Moses because he was in a sinful relationship. After they speak and exalt themselves, the Bible declares, *"And the Lord heard it"* (Numbers 12:2). Wow! God was listening in on their conversation. He heard when they spoke against their leader.

God still hears today. He isn't pleased when we speak bad of our leaders, even if the fault is a serious one. We are not to judge. God is using them and will continue to do so.

I'm not saying that you should follow a leader who's living in blatant sin. Nor should we do everything a leader tells us to do if it causes us to sin. However, we have no right to speak against a leader God has placed above us.

Something very severe happened to Miriam. I believe this shows the severity of talking against a leader and how God feels about it.

> *So the anger of the Lord burned against them and He departed. But when the cloud had withdrawn from over the tent, behold, Miriam was leprous, as white as snow.*
> —Numbers 12:9–10

God's reaction may seem harsh, but He hates sin. Thankfully, He dealt with sin once and for all on the cross of Jesus. The price of sin has been paid for. God, however, has included these stories in the Old Testament for us to learn from them. They show us how sin affects our lives.

Let's be cautious about speaking against or participating in conversation that belittles our leaders. Be humble and don't open the door of slander. It's not worth it.

Trusting God's Timing

Do you want to see God move in mighty ways? Do you want to be the best leader you can be? If so, be faithful and learn from others. I can't stress the importance of faithfulness enough. Don't worry about how long it will take; simply be faithful and God will open doors of opportunity for you.

STAND THE TEST OF TIME

chapter two

As we examine the heroes of faith in the Bible, we can see that each one had to stand the test of time. We often sit and read the Bible superficially, without studying it or seeing all the truths God has for us. We're quick to skim the surface of stories we've heard before instead of asking God to take us deeper and teach us something new. We read the stories in fifteen to twenty minutes and don't really comprehend how many years these people walked with God before receiving their promise. Oh how we can learn from the people who went before us!

If we continue in this way, we'll never understand what it is to wait for the promises of God—and to enjoy walking with God through the process. We'll never see that we need to have *"faith and patience [to] inherit the promises"* (Hebrews 6:12). It's too easy in our culture of instant gratification to give up on anything and everyone if things don't go the way we want, when we want. We want everything on our own timetable, but we have to trust heaven's timing. We need to realize that God's working behind the scenes.

Time and patience are two words we don't often like to hear. In our fast-paced day, we want everything as soon as possible. We want fast food and microwave dinners, email, smartphones, and apps for online banking—anything that will help us get things done quicker. We don't appreciate it when we hear "You'll have to wait a while. Please be patient." We want to hear "We'll be right with you. It'll only take a second!"

And we want the blessings of God to come to us in the same way, but God isn't the God of instant gratification. We read in the Bible, *"Blessed be the God and Father of our Lord Jesus Christ, who has blessed us with every spiritual blessing in the heavenly places in Christ"* (Ephesians 1:3). The great news is that it's a done deal. He's already blessed us. We don't have to work for His blessings because Christ paid the price so we would be blessed. However, we don't always walk in the full blessings of God as we could. Like all Scripture, we need to line ourselves up with it. We need to position ourselves to receive what God's already given to us. When we don't see the blessings come as we would like, we shouldn't blame God. Rather, we must look to see why we aren't receiving our blessings.

It's God's desire to bless you. You're His child and He wants the best for you. He's got His best intentions for you. We need to understand this before we endeavour to do things for Him. I'm saying all this because many times God's blessing is right before our eyes, but because circumstances cloud our vision, we back out right before receiving it.

When we don't seem to receive our blessing right away, most of the time it's because God's still working in us, preparing us. When God gives you a vision for your life, it won't be fulfilled in an instant. You'll have to wait for it. God will work in your life so your character matches with His. He wants to make us into His image. His highest calling is that we would be like Him in all we do, and who we are.

It hurts me to see so many people giving up before the promise comes to pass. After counselling many people, seeing their struggles and experiencing my own, I've seen that the wait trips us up. It can suck the very life out of us, if we allow it to. If you feel like you've been waiting a long time to get your answer from God, don't worry; others have waited longer. God is always faithful to fulfill His promises in His timing.

One scripture that encourages me is in the book of Joshua, where we see that if God's going to give a promise, He will fulfill it, even if it takes forty years or more.

Not one of the good promises which the Lord had made to the house of Israel failed; all came to pass.
—Joshua 21:45

What an amazing word to us! We need to remember this on a daily basis. If God fulfilled all the promises He gave to the Israelites, why wouldn't He do the same for us? Let's choose to believe, even though it seems like we've been believing forever without even a hint of the promise coming to pass. We need to believe even if it seems that things are only getting worse.

Let's first go to the man who started it all, the one whom we call the father of faith. We can learn so much from his life.

Abram's full story only takes up twelve chapters of the Bible, and if we don't read them carefully we may not realize how long Abram had to wait to see his promise from God come to pass. Here's the promise God gives to Abram:

Now the Lord said to Abram, "Go forth from your country, and from your relatives and from your father's house, to the land which I will show you; and I will make you a great nation, and I will bless you, and make your name great; and so you shall be a blessing; and I will bless those who bless you, and the one who curses you I will curse. And in you all the families of the earth will be blessed."

—Genesis 12:1–3

What an enormous promise—all the families on earth were going to be blessed by him! But first he had to take some steps of obedience. He had to leave the place where his family lived. He may have been comfortable there, but God wanted to make him into someone different, first by taking him somewhere different. He was promised that if he left and went to this place he didn't know, God would make a great nation out of him, bless him, and make his name great. On top of all that, God would bless the people who blessed him and curse the people who cursed him. That sounds pretty good to me. I would want that to happen right away, as soon as I left the country in my obedience to God.

God's promise to make of Abram a great nation seems farfetched. Abram didn't have a single child and he was getting old. How was God going to make a great nation out of him? Abram needed to have faith in God if he was going to believe Him for this promise.

When God gives us a dream or a vision, it's always much bigger than we are; we can't fulfill it in our own strength. God wants us to completely depend on Him for the great things He wants to do in our lives. Dare to dream big! God doesn't get scared when you dream big for Him. God's vision for your life is bigger than you've ever imagined. Ask Him to show it to you. He can do even greater than you could even think to ask (Ephesians 3:20).

Stand the Test of Time

So Abram went forth as the Lord had spoken to him; and Lot went with him. Now Abram was seventy-five years old when he departed from Haran.

—Genesis 12:4

Abram kept his part of the deal. He left his country. However, he brought a family member along with him. God would deal with that mistake later, but He at least got Abram to the place where He wanted him.

There's a big clue here. Abram was seventy-five years old when he left for the country of promise. As we look at the story, we'll see how much time actually went by for Abram to receive God's promises. I believe that God included these timeframes so we won't grow faint and give up while waiting for His promises to us.

First, Abram needed to separate from his nephew, Lot. They were both very rich and the land couldn't hold the two of them plus their livestock and other material possessions. We see God's favour upon Abram as he accumulated wealth. However, God wanted complete obedience before he could bring about the promise. Abram needed to get rid of his extra baggage.

What baggage is God asking you to get rid of before the promise He gave you can come to pass? What has God been asking you to change in order to be in complete obedience to Him? He needs you to let it go.

As we grow in grace and throw away the baggage that's holding us back, God shows us the vision in greater detail. He brings His plans to a greater and more specific revelation. Look at what God says to Abram after Lot was gone:

The Lord said to Abram, after Lot had separated from him, "Now lift up your eyes and look from the place where you are, northward and southward and eastward and westward; for all the land which you see, I will give it to you and to your descendants forever. I will make your descendants as the dust of the earth, so that if anyone can number the dust of the earth, then your descendants can also be numbered. Arise, walk about the land through its length and breadth; for I will give it to you."

—Genesis 13:14–17

As you see, God didn't speak to Abram about the vision again until he had separated from Lot. Once he was gone, God had him envision the whole land he was promised, and all the descendants needed to fill it. This must have seemed incredible, since Abram still didn't have a child and was pushing eighty years old. Abram had to envision the promise before he could walk it through. We can't just envision what God has told us; we also need to physically walk it out.

My wife Karla and I saw the land for City of Refuge before we bought it, but we also needed to walk it out and proclaim that God had given us the land, and then we received it. You need to walk in faith, knowing that if God has promised it, He will definitely fulfill it for you.

The vision must have seemed overwhelming at times. Abraham must have thought, *God, you had better start right away or you won't be able to do this because I'm too old already!* The vision often seems so big that we won't be able to finish it in our lifetimes, but we can if we trust Him and His calling.

Abram saw a good part of his vision fulfilled, but he didn't see the complete expansion through his lineage, the generations that would come after him, and Jesus the Messiah, who was the ultimate fulfillment of the promise. He didn't see the followers of Jesus, his children by faith. The vision was much bigger than even he could have imagined.

Stand the Test of Time

Karla and I also believe that the City of Refuge will outlast us. It will go on to bless more people than we could ever hope for.

When God gives a vision, it's meant to be eternal. He wants us to train up others who can run with the vision long after we're gone. That's why God wants us to raise up disciples, people who will follow Him as we do.

Throughout Abram's faith journey, God had to reaffirm many times that He was going to do what He said He would. But as the years passed, Abram wasn't seeing anything of the vision or words God had spoken. If he were going to have descendants to fill the land of Canaan, wouldn't he need at least one son? Nothing of this vision made sense to Abram. Things didn't seem to progress at all. Instead of getting closer, he felt further away.

When Karla and I began to look for land, because we knew God had spoken to us about the City of Refuge, it often seemed like we were close, but then we'd experience a disappointing setback and the promise would seem further away than before. What we thought would happen in a short time stretched out into a five-year journey of faith.

We found one plot of land we liked and were ready to buy it when we found out that it had a $60,000 lien on it. We would have bought into that debt if we hadn't looked into things first. Then some people wanted to sell us different land, but they tripled the price when we were ready to close the deal. It seemed like we just kept hitting dead ends. We wondered if God was really going to give us what He had promised. At times it seemed so far away. Other times it seemed so close, but the next step only ended in frustration and discouragement.

This is why I believe God's timing is so important. We must realize that when God gives us a vision, He also knows exactly when it will be fulfilled. According to Isaiah 46:10,

Trusting God's Timing

"Declaring the end from the beginning... saying, 'My purpose will be established, and I will accomplish all My good pleasure.'"

There's no need for us to worry and think that God isn't going to come through for us. We have to trust that the vision will come to pass in His timing! God knew before He gave us the vision how long it would take to come to pass. It's we who believe there's a different timeframe, but we need to continually trust God.

Looking back, I can see how God was preparing us every step of the way. Every time there was a disappointment or setback, it was just God saying it wasn't time yet. We had more to learn and we needed the time for God to teach us. We weren't ready for what was to come. God wanted to prepare our hearts before He gave us the great task that was before us. If we had pushed, we would have given birth to an Ishmael—and we didn't want to do that. We wanted to know that we were in God's perfect will and timing.

Speaking of Ishmael, let's look at what happened when Abram and his wife Sarai became impatient and tried to give God a hand to speed things up. It's so easy to fall into this trap. Let's learn from their experience.

> *Now Sarai, Abram's wife had borne him no children, and she had an Egyptian maid whose name was Hagar. So Sarai said to Abram, "Now behold, the Lord has prevented me from bearing children. Please go in to my maid; perhaps I will obtain children through her." And Abram listened to the voice of Sarai. After Abram had lived ten years in the land of Canaan, Abram's wife Sarai took Hagar the Egyptian, her maid, and gave her to her husband Abram as his wife. He went in to Hagar, and she conceived; and when she saw that she had conceived, her mistress was despised in her sight.*
> —Genesis 16:1–4

Stand the Test of Time

In this passage, we see that ten years had passed since Abraham moved to the land of Canaan. He was now eighty-five years old. What a long time to wait! He had seen no sign of the vision coming to pass and he and Sarai kept getting older. Surely, we can understand why they might have started thinking they needed to help God out.

Like Sarai, through human reasoning we often rationalize that God can't do what He promised. If we stare at the natural circumstances, we won't be able to see the supernatural. If we focus on how impossible things are, we'll never see the power of God. We have to take our eyes off our circumstances and just believe God for what He's said.

Abram and Sarai made a huge mistake by thinking to give God a hand. God doesn't need us to help Him with the vision He's given us. He gave it to us knowing what circumstances we were going to face and how long it would take to fulfill the vision. God already knows how He's going to bring it to pass, so we don't need to worry. We need to trust in Him. There's no other way.

Thank God that He doesn't just leave us when we make mistakes. He doesn't just say, "Okay, you screwed up. I can't work with you any longer. I had great things lined up for you, but you messed it up." No, God always has a plan.

God knew Abram would make his mistake. God still showed His love towards Abram, and He will do the same for you. His love and mercy are everlasting.

Take a few minutes to thank God for not giving up on you. Even though you've blown it many times, He still loves you. He'll still lead and guide you onto the right path. He knew where you would be today. He's ready to even bless your mistake, as He did for Abram.

As for Ishmael, I have heard you; behold, I will bless him, and will make him fruitful and will multiply him exceedingly. He shall become the father of twelve princes, and I will make him a great nation.

—Genesis 17:20

God was going to take Abram's mistake and use it to fulfill His purposes. God even said He would bring twelve princes from Ishmael's lineage. God's a merciful God. Never think that God can't use you because you've made a few mistakes. Get back up and see God move through you again. He will allow you learn from your mistake so you don't make it again.

I want you to see something in the Scriptures that we often overlook. As we're reading stories, we don't always pay attention to the timeframe. Let's look at two verses that show a gap in time.

Abram was eighty-six years old when Hagar bore Ishmael to him. Now when Abram was ninety-nine years old, the Lord appeared to Abram and said to him...

—Genesis 16:16–17:1

Between these two verses, thirteen years pass that we know nothing about. We don't get a glimpse as to what happened. Maybe Abram needed these thirteen years to learn from his mistake. He could have been in repentance. We really don't know. All we know is that many years went by that don't seem to have been important enough to write about. There were thirteen years of silence before God came with an even clearer picture of what was about to happen.

Now when Abram was ninety-nine years old, the Lord appeared to Abram and said to him, "I am God Almighty; walk before Me, and be blameless. I will establish My covenant between Me and you, and I will multiply you exceedingly."

Abram fell on his face, and God talked with him, saying, "As for Me, behold, My covenant is with you, and you will be the father of a multitude of nations. No longer shall your name be called Abram, but your name shall be Abraham; for I have made you the father of a multitude of nations.

"I will make you exceedingly fruitful, and I will make nations of you, and kings will come forth from you. I will establish My covenant between Me and you and your descendants after you throughout their generations for an everlasting covenant, to be God to you and to your descendants after you. I will give to you and to your descendants after you, the land of your sojournings, all the land of Canaan, for an everlasting possession; and I will be their God."

—Genesis 17:1–8

Here, God announces to Abram what's about to happen. God shows him the greatness of the vision twenty-four years earlier. Abram had to wait a long time, he made some mistakes along the way, and there were thirteen years of silence, but then God provided a powerful revelation of what He would do through Abram.

God announces that He'll make a covenant with Abram and his descendants and he will be the father of a multitude of nations. For this, God changes Abram's name to Abraham, which means "father of many." God then talks about the significant people who will come from Abraham. God's vision gets clearer and more focused. God's going to do something of great importance in Abraham's life; now he has to prepare for it.

If we read ahead just a bit, we see that God also gives a timeframe. Abraham may have wished that God had told him in the beginning how long it would take. If only God had given Abraham a heads up, maybe he wouldn't have made so many mistakes.

As we train ourselves to hear God's voice and walk toward the vision He gave us, His voice will become clearer and His direction will become more exact.

Then God gives a name to the child: *"But My covenant I will establish with Isaac, whom Sarah will bear to you at this season next year"* (Genesis 17:21). Isaac was going to bring laughter, which is what his name means. There was going to be a certain joy about this child. God also says that the birth of the child would come to pass in one year's time.

When the vision God has given you comes to fruition, great joy and laughter comes with it. All your dreams, everything you were waiting for, just drops into place. You see that your hope wasn't in vain. God's been with you the whole time, every step of the way.

> *Hope deferred makes a heart sick, but desire fulfilled is a tree of life.*
>
> —Proverbs 13:12

When we dedicated the land for City of Refuge, we weren't the only ones who were joyful; many people around us wanted to see the vision come to pass. We thought we would be the only people truly happy about it, but at the celebration service people began to dance and rejoice in the presence of God. It was a time of laughter and happiness. The vision had been birthed and our ministry begun.

This is why I can encourage you today to believe for God's vision to come to pass. I, too, had to go through years of waiting and wondering. I experienced times of discouragement and things seemed distant, but once the vision came to

Stand the Test of Time

pass, our laughter and joy were contagious. God wants to do the same for you. He wants to bring you to a place of rejoicing!

God had to change Abraham and Sarah's names so they would speak faith to one another. Abraham needed to be called the father of many so he could see it. He needed to call Sarah his princess so that she could believe it. It's so important to speak God's Word to one another as you believe for something. Encourage one another on a daily basis.

People may have wondered why Sarah called Abraham a father of many, since they didn't even have a child together. When he introduced himself as Abraham, the father of many, and was asked how many children he had, he would have to respond with, "Only Ishmael. I don't have any children with Sarah at this time, but I will. I'm almost one hundred years old, but just wait and see."

Faith requires us to act and speak things forth. We must speak what we believe in our hearts. Faith changes the way we speak and the words we use. When God speaks to us, we must speak His words of life into our situations, even if everything around us screams differently. Hold on to your confession. Know that God's going to do what He promised. If He did it for Abraham, He'll do it for you.

Next, we're going to look at Genesis 21. Remember how thirteen years passed in just two verses earlier? Then it takes four chapters to explain what happened in the following year of believing for the vision. I find it of great value to realize how many years went by, especially when we're impatient and don't know why things haven't happened when we expected.

Then came what was one of the best days of Abraham's life. He finally got to physically touch the vision. He no longer only saw it though faith, but it was tangible. God fulfilled the promise.

Trusting God's Timing

Then the Lord took note of Sarah as He had said, and the Lord did for Sarah as He had promised. So Sarah conceived and bore a son to Abraham in his old age, at the appointed time of which God had spoken to him. Abraham called the name of his son who was born to him, whom Sarah bore to him, Isaac. Then Abraham circumcised his son Isaac when he was eight days old, as God had commanded him. Now Abraham was one hundred years old when his son Isaac was born to him.
—Genesis 21:1–5

They were now holding the long-awaited promise in their arms. Again, God mentions how old Abraham was: one hundred years old. When God gave Abraham the original vision, he was seventy-five years old, so it took *twenty-five* years for God to bring to pass what He had promised.

It may have seemed long to Abraham, but it didn't take long for God to accomplish the vision. We are so limited by time and space that we can't see the way God sees. God can see outside of time. He created time for us. Let's not be scared by it. We shouldn't worry about the length of time it takes to see the vision come about. We need to rest knowing that God will fulfill His promises.

Maybe you've been waiting for two, five, twenty, or fifty years; it really doesn't matter how long. God has given you the promise. He knows the timeframe that it will take him to accomplish it. He's not worried about that, and neither should you. Rest in God, knowing that it is His promise and He will make sure it comes to pass.

If God fulfilled His promises before, He will do the same for us today. Hebrews 13:8 says, *"Jesus Christ is the same yesterday and today and forever."* Shake off all doubt and worry. God is fighting for you behind the scenes. You can't see it, but rest assured that He is.

HARDSHIPS COME TO MAKE US STRONGER

chapter three

Joseph is another person who had a long wait before he saw his dream fulfilled. He had to go through many years of trials and discouragement before seeing the fullness of God's plans. He didn't expect it to take as long as it did. I'm sure he shared his dream with his family because he believed it was going to happen soon. Joseph had bold faith that he would see what God had shown him in the dream.

Joseph was like many young people today. He suffered rejection and betrayal, but he was still willing to believe God. He had his Father's love and approval. Joseph was able at a young age to see past his difficulties and know that God was going to do something great in his life. He believed that he was going to be someone of importance and do something of great significance.

Let's look closely at Joseph's life to learn from his mistakes and the things he had to go through. We need to see how our circumstances prepare us for God's call. This way, we'll never think that we're too far from God's plan for our lives. We'll always know that He's with us, even at our lowest point.

We need to start in Genesis 37:2 to read about when Joseph first received the dream. The Bible tells us that he was seventeen years old. At this young age, he had a dream of greatness. God was going to do something awesome in his life. Today we would say something like, "Joseph knew that he was going to be a world-shaker and a history-maker." He was on fire and wanted to be used by God!

Joseph had his father's approval. We even see that Joseph was his father's favourite. Let's take a look what it was like for Joseph in his family:

> *Now Israel loved Joseph more than all his sons, because he was the son of his old age; and he made him a varicolored tunic. His brothers saw that their father loved him more than all his brothers; and so they hated him and could not speak to him on friendly terms.*
>
> —Genesis 37:3–4

This is one sad family. I hope you don't have to experience what happens when a parent loves one child more than his or her siblings. It was painfully obvious that Israel loved Joseph more than his brothers—everyone in the family could see it. This caused overwhelming strife and jealousy. How sad it would be if you couldn't speak to your own brothers because they hated you.

Joseph must have seen that he was hated. His brothers couldn't speak kindly to him. Perhaps he was naïve and didn't see that this wouldn't be a good time to brag and share his dream of greatness. Why would you share your dream with people who are jealous of you and can't even speak kindly to you? Why would you tell them that you would rise above them? Obviously, the listeners wouldn't receive your news with joy and gladness. They wouldn't celebrate your dream with you.

However, in the following verses, we can see the immaturity on Joseph's part. The dream had been just between him and God. It wasn't supposed to be released just yet.

Hardships Come to Make Us Stronger

Then Joseph had a dream, and when he told it to his brothers, they hated him even more. He said to them, "Please listen to this dream which I have had; for behold, we were binding sheaves in the field, and lo, my sheaf rose up and also stood erect; and behold, your sheaves gathered around and bowed down to my sheaf."

—Genesis 37:5–7

Obviously Joseph's brothers didn't take this dream very well since they hated him even more. He was telling the very people who were already jealous of him that one day they would bow down to him, that he was going to be of much more importance than they, that eventually they would recognize his authority.

Some dreams aren't meant to be discussed. We need to be mature enough to know when and who we can share our dreams with. Deciding to broadcast them to everyone can produce hardships that could otherwise be avoided. We can learn from Joseph's life. We must learn when to keep our mouths shut and when it's the time to release what God has shown us in our quiet times with Him.

God gave Joseph yet another dream in which even his parents bowed down to him (Genesis 37:9–11). As if the reaction to the first dream wasn't bad enough, Joseph blurted it out again, apparently not learning from his mistake. He had to rub it in. He had to be a big shot.

We have to realize that when God plants a seed of greatness inside us, it's nothing to boast about. It shouldn't puff us up with pride. God's simply showing us what He wants to do in our lives, and when He does it, He will receive the glory. In the Kingdom of Heaven, we're to be the least in order to be the greatest. We need to humble ourselves so we will be exalted (Luke 14:11).

We are part of His Kingdom, where we must seek to be servants. We don't seek fame and fortune. We seek God's Kingdom. It's okay to have a seed of greatness inside of us, knowing that God put it there, but we must not boast. We should reflect on it and thank God that He's entrusted it to us and remember how dependent we are to have Him bring it to pass. We're all great in God's eyes. God has placed a seed of greatness inside all of us. We should never look down on others; we should see the greatness God has placed in them as well.

We see some interesting things happen in Joseph's story. First, his brothers sell him into slavery—an abrupt assault on his feeling of importance (Genesis 37:25–28). He went from being a person of high status to low status in a moment. However, Joseph's faith seems to pull him through any hardship. He knows that God can still make his dream come to pass.

Here's where a lot of us fail. We see the hardship and focus on all the trouble that happens to us. Instead of going forward, we seem to move backward, making no progress at all. We take one step forward only to take two steps back. We begin to believe the lies of the enemy that we don't have a call from God, that we're worthless and there's nothing God can do.

God wants to show us, however, that even in hardships, we're in the centre of His will. When circumstances are tough, God's still in it with us. The Holy Spirit is still inside us and God's going to make His plans come to pass. We have to learn from these circumstances. Many times we're still growing and God wants to teach us things and work on our character. As others have said before, it took God a day to get the Israelites out of Egypt, but it took forty years to get Egypt out of them. They needed to see that God had a better plan for them. They wanted to go back to Egypt because it looked better (Exodus 14:12). God, however, saw the bigger picture. We must look to God to see this bigger picture as well.

Hardships Come to Make Us Stronger

We need to take our eyes off of our problems and look to Jesus. We need to settle in our hearts that God's dream will come to pass no matter how dark our situation is. However difficult the hardship may seem, God's still with us. Allow God to deposit His seed of greatness so deeply inside you that you know He's going to turn things around. He did it for Joseph and He'll definitely do it for you.

> *Now Joseph had been taken down to Egypt; and Potiphar, an Egyptian officer of Pharaoh, the captain of the bodyguard, bought him from the Ishmaelites, who had taken him down there. The Lord was with Joseph, so he became a successful man. And he was in the house of his master, the Egyptian. Now his master saw that the Lord was with him and how the Lord caused all that he did to prosper in his hand. So Joseph found favor in his sight and became his personal servant; and he made him overseer over his house, and all that he owned he put in his charge. It came about that from the time he made him overseer in his house and over all that he owned, the Lord blessed the Egyptian's house on account of Joseph; thus the Lord's blessing was upon all that he owned, in the house and in the field. So he left everything he owned in Joseph's charge; and with him there he did not concern himself with anything except the food which he ate.*
> —Genesis 39:1–6

Wait a minute. Wasn't Joseph sold into slavery? Wasn't this to be one of the lowest positions? This, my friend, is God's grace in action. Here's God stepping in right in the midst of hardships. Even though Joseph was going through the hardest time in his life to this point, God reminded him that he had a seed of greatness inside. Once again, Joseph had an ounce of hope that he would be the leader the Lord had called him to be.

Trusting God's Timing

I think Joseph was getting excited. He could see that God was on his side. In fact, even the unbelieving Potiphar could see that God was with Joseph. Potiphar took notice of how God blessed everything Joseph did and couldn't think of anything wiser than to put Joseph in charge of everything he owned. Here was Joseph, a slave, yet very successful. It was so obvious that even unbelievers began to take notice.

Joseph must have thought this was his big break. He was rising to greatness and, one day, his brothers would bow their knees to him. It seemed as if success was right around the corner. His blessing was sure to come. His hardships had finally come to an end—or had they?

In the midst of Joseph's rising, an unfortunate thing happened: a false accusation against him caused him to fall back to the bottom. Potiphar's wife harassed Joseph daily, trying to convince him to have sex with her. He refused, instead did the right thing, and yet another hardship came his way. He was thrown into jail because Potiphar's wife made it seem like Joseph had tried to rape her (Genesis 38:7–20).

Everything had been looking up. He had risen quite high on the scale of importance. Things finally looked like they were turning around, and then wham! One false accusation and Joseph was done in Potiphar's house. Even though he did what was right, he still faced hardship and opposition.

Joseph had a choice to make. Was he going to let discouragement break him or continue to believe God and what He had shown him? He chose not to get bitter. He was going to hold on to the promises God had given him and not let this hardship shake his faith. He proved that he could stand the test of time, and so should we. We need to look at this story closely and realize that God's been with us the whole time, and He'll continue to be with us even in our dark times.

Hardships Come to Make Us Stronger

Before we go on with Joseph's story, I want to share something similar that happened at House of Refuge. In 2002, God gave me a vision that I would reach out to alcoholics, drug addicts, and prostitutes and see them touched, changed, and transformed by God's power. The vision was so powerful that it seemed like God was going to do something right away.

I began to talk with different pastors and leaders about this vision. Some of them received the vision, while others thought it wasn't worthwhile to reach out to these types of people. I decided not to get discouraged and instead work with the people who were excited about the vision. I began to minister on the streets of Chiquimulilla and saw a definite hunger for God.

However, it took two years before we saw any fruit.

Week after week, I preached to these men and women and no one gave their heart to Jesus. The people working alongside me became weary and discouraged. Some began to ask me if I wouldn't rather work with children, since they would be more grateful for the things I gave them. My only response was that God hadn't called me to the children, but to alcoholics, drug addicts, and prostitutes.

Since those who had helped were no longer willing, I decided to ask some of my best friends to help. They were excited to do so at the beginning. We began the ministry and things really began to take off. Many people got saved, healed, and delivered. God was moving in powerful ways.

We saw so much victory, it was awesome. I also met my wife Karla at this time, and we got married one year later. The miracles and salvations continued. After we married, Juan Ramon came to House of Refuge and was saved and healed. (For more of his story, read my book *What Will You Give to Jesus?*) It seemed like God was starting a revival among the street men.

As we continued to see more men come to live in the House of Refuge and come through recovery, we thought the whole vision God had given us was finally coming to pass. That's when God gave Karla and me a fresh vision for what we call the City of Refuge. This would take our ministry to a whole new level. Not only would we house men and give them a place to stay, now they would commit to a one-year term to help them down the road of recovery and teach them new trades.

We prepared for the vision. Because we seemed so close to seeing what God had shown us, we began looking for land to build on and looked forward to what was going to happen next.

Then something very heart-rending happened. Our best friends, who had been helping start the ministry, started to make false accusations about us to the very men we were ministering to. They lied about us and made us out to be bad people. The lies and accusations became so intense that we had to dismiss our friends immediately, leaving us with no one to help.

It was a hard decision to make, but we knew it was the right one. We continued to see God move. He was with us this whole time. However, it was a hit we weren't expecting. We weren't ready for our best friends to backstab us and make us out to be bad people. We had to learn to forgive and put these things behind us. We were able to do so and have seen God turn this sad story into an incredible testimony.

Like Joseph, we thought God's timing was right around the corner. It seemed like the climax was near. Yet God said we still had so much to learn. We still needed to grow and get ready for what was about to happen. It was a new season in ministry

It's so important that we see the ups and the downs as part of God's plan.

But the Lord was with Joseph and extended kindness to him, and gave him favor in the sight of the chief jailer. The

chief jailer committed to Joseph's charge all the prisoners who were in the jail; so that whatever was done there, he was responsible for it. The chief jailer did not supervise anything under Joseph's charge because the Lord was with him; and whatever he did, the Lord made to prosper.
—Genesis 39:21–23

Do we really understand this? Here Joseph is made a prisoner for the false accusations that were made against him. He's locked up with the lowest of the low. It seems like things couldn't get any worse. Thank God that He can use us even in the darkest situations. God can make a way where there seems to be no way.

Joseph was so well-behaved and at rest in God's promises that he received favour from the chief jailer. He was probably the only prisoner who did what he was told, who acted in obedience, and respected everyone there. So great was the difference that the chief jailer knew he could trust Joseph. The chief jailer didn't even supervise him because he knew Joseph was an upright man. Even though accusations had come against Joseph, people around him could see that he was different and the accusations weren't true. He didn't need to defend himself; he simply trusted that God had a plan, even in the prison cell.

In these scriptures, *"the Lord was with Joseph and extended kindness to him"* (Genesis 39:21). This had to have been God.

I worked for a couple of years in prison ministry and I never saw a prisoner given authority in any way. I never witnessed a single case of a prisoner not needing to be supervised. It just doesn't happen. If you're in jail, whether it's due to false accusation or not, you're going to pay. Justice will be served. For Joseph to receive such authority and be given so much trust, it had to be God's doing.

Trusting God's Timing

God knew Joseph's heart. He also knew Joseph was innocent and had a plan for his life. God wasn't going to give up on Joseph at his lowest point. He was going to prepare him for what He had planned for him. God called Joseph to be a leader, so his gifting was evident even in prison. It didn't matter where he was, his gift of leadership shone. Why? He was sure of his calling and knew God had called him to be a leader.

At this point, Joseph must have felt overwhelming discouragement from his fellow prisoners. He must have had times when he thought he would never leave prison and would be there for the rest of his life. However, Joseph decided to put his confidence in God. He knew God had called him and that God is a good God. With confidence, he could face any storm or hardship ahead of him.

You and I need to have this same confidence. We need to know who we are in Christ. The fact that God has called us for a special purpose needs to be so instilled in us that we don't let anyone steal our dream. We must not let others discourage us. We must not allow people, because of their jealousy, to bring us down. At all times we must look to Him who has called us. We must draw our strength from God. Once we do this, we can face any hardship or difficult circumstance. Once it's settled in our hearts that God's a good God all the time, then and only then can we walk in the assurance that God will work everything together for our good. He will bring us from the pit to His place of favour and use us for His glory.

Joseph's is a story of many ups and downs. This is probably why we can relate to it so well. While he's still a prisoner, his life turns around. You see, God was doing more than refining Joseph's character; He was positioning him for an important connection. At this time, Joseph meets two more prisoners who are troubled by dreams. Joseph had another gifting that's about to be seen—the gift of dream interpretation. Eventually, God uses this gift to bring him out of the prison and raise him into a place of leadership. However, God doesn't do it quickly, even though He could have. He takes His time to bring it to pass.

The two prisoners were important men in Pharaoh's palace. One was Pharaoh's cupbearer and the other his chief baker. Joseph was able to interpret their troubling dreams. Once Joseph gave the interpretation to the cupbearer—the man's dream meant that he was going to get his position back—the chief baker also wanted to hear the interpretation of his dream. However, his interpretation wasn't favourable. The baker was going to be killed rather than put back into his position (Genesis 40:22–24).

After Joseph interpreted the dream of the cupbearer, he asked him for one simple favour. He wanted the cupbearer to mention him to Pharaoh.

> *Only keep me in mind when it goes well with you, and please do me a kindness by mentioning me to Pharaoh and get me out of this house. For I was in fact kidnapped from the land of the Hebrews, and even here I have done nothing that they should have put me into the dungeon.*
> —Genesis 40:14–15

What a simple thing for Joseph to ask. This cupbearer was going to be by Pharaoh's side every day, having access to him because of his job. The cupbearer would bring all beverages to Pharaoh, and even try some first to make sure no one was trying to kill Pharaoh. It was an important job that involved a lot of trust.

After the cupbearer was presented to Pharaoh and given his position back, you would think one of the first things he'd do is mention Joseph. How could he forget such a simple favour for the man who had brought him such encouragement while he was in prison? However, it appears that the cupbearer did just that. The Bible declares, *"Yet the chief cupbearer did not remember Joseph, but forgot him"* Genesis 40:23).

Joseph remained in prison. He had no way to get out and remind the cupbearer of his situation. He could only pray for God to remind him. He had nowhere else to put his confidence. He needed to believe God would move.

I'm sure he wondered every day if this would be the day. He must have waited patiently, wondering at what hour he would be released. He waited and waited and waited. We don't hear much of what happened in this time, but we do hear how long he waited: *"Now it happened at the end of two full years that Pharaoh had a dream…"* (Genesis 41:1)

Two full years passed and nothing was done for Joseph. No one came to rescue him out of prison. He had been forgotten once again.

The pain of rejection continued. Here he had thought his time had come, that he was going to be let out, yet he had to wait two full years. How many of us today would survive in prison two extra years for a crime we didn't commit? We become quickly discouraged and give up on God. Not Joseph; he knew that he served a good God.

The Bible goes on to share two dreams Pharaoh had. He couldn't figure out what they meant and he had no one to interpret them. He asked everyone around and became desperate. At that moment, the cupbearer remembered Joseph and how he had interpreted his dream. He then recalled the favour Joseph had asked of him two years earlier.

> *Then the chief cupbearer spoke to Pharaoh, saying, "I would make mention today of my own offenses. Pharaoh was furious with his servants, and he put me in confinement in the house of the captain of the bodyguard, both me and the*

chief baker. We had a dream on the same night, he and I; each of us dreamed according to the interpretation of his own dream. Now a Hebrew youth was with us there, a servant of the captain of the bodyguard, and we related them to him, and he interpreted our dreams for us. To each one he interpreted according to his own dream. And just as he interpreted for us, so it happened; he restored me in my office, but he hanged him."

—Genesis 41:9–13

God gave Pharaoh those dreams. The cupbearer may have forgotten about Joseph, but God hadn't. God made sure there was no way this man could keep quiet. If he had forgotten once, God would make it so he wouldn't forget again.

This was a whole new day for Joseph, one he would never forget. In prison, he received the call he had been waiting for: Pharaoh wanted to see him. Although I'm sure he wasn't prepared for what was about to happen, the time had come for God to raise him up. Joseph had gone through enough hardships and God's plan was about to unfold.

Joseph would have been happy with just getting out of prison. Well, wouldn't you be? But God had been preparing him for greatness this whole time.

Then Pharaoh sent and called for Joseph, and they hurriedly brought him out of the dungeon; and when he had shaved himself and changed his clothes, he came to Pharaoh.
—Genesis 41:14

On this day, the one Joseph longed for, he quickly changed and made himself presentable to stand before Pharaoh. He didn't delay for one minute. He knew he hadn't done anything wrong and he was sure God was with him. If Pharaoh

Trusting God's Timing

had called for him, it had to be for a good reason. After all, Joseph knew God still loved him and had a plan for his life. The plan had to be fulfilled. Joseph had nothing to fear and he wasn't going to let his time in jail allow him to rot in bitterness. Rather, he was confident in his calling and no one could have persuaded him otherwise.

Don't let anyone talk you out of your calling. If God has called you, He will bring it to pass. He will make all things possible. Even when times are tough and it looks like there's no way out, God still has a plan. He's in control. We can put our complete confidence in Him. This is how we'll see our dreams fulfilled. We need to be steadfast in our calling. Know that every trial you face further prepares you for the calling God has placed on your life.

Pharaoh shared his dreams with Joseph. Joseph listened to both dreams and God revealed to him the interpretation:

It is as I have spoken to Pharaoh: God has shown to Pharaoh what He is about to do. Behold, seven years of great abundance are coming in all the land of Egypt; and after them seven years of famine will come, and all the abundance will be forgotten in the land of Egypt, and the famine will ravage the land. So the abundance will be unknown in the land because of that subsequent famine; for it will be very severe.

—Genesis 41:28–31

This is where Joseph's story gets even more exciting. Straight out of prison, he was lifted by God to the place He had spoken to him about so many years before. Joseph knew he had an important role to play in this life. People, even his family, would bow down to him. But now he knew it was nothing to boast about. The authority came with great responsibilities to care for those under him. He hadn't seen that when he was young and thought it was going to happen right away. God had other plans. God didn't reveal all the steps it would take. He never does.

> *Now as for the repeating of the dream to Pharaoh twice, it means that the matter is determined by God, and God will quickly bring it about. Now let Pharaoh look for a man discerning and wise, and set him over the land of Egypt. Let Pharaoh take action to appoint overseers in charge of the land, and let him exact a fifth of the produce of the land of Egypt in the seven years of abundance. Then let them gather all the food of these good years that are coming, and store up the grain for food in the cities under Pharaoh's authority, and let them guard it. Let the food become as a reserve for the land for the seven years of famine which will occur in the land of Egypt, so that the land will not perish during the famine.*
>
> —Genesis 41:32–36

After Joseph interpreted Pharaoh's dream, he gave Pharaoh some advice on what to do. He had God's wisdom and knew how to solve the problem before anyone asked him. This proves his great leadership skills. He didn't see the problem; he saw the solution. This was the solution God used to catapult him from prisoner to second-in-command, Pharaoh's right-hand man.

> *Now the proposal seemed good to Pharaoh and to all his servants.*
>
> *Then Pharaoh said to his servants, "Can we find a man like this, in whom is a divine spirit?" So Pharaoh said*

to Joseph, "Since God has informed you of all this, there is no one so discerning and wise as you are. You shall be over my house, and according to your command all my people shall do homage; only in the throne I will be greater than you." Pharaoh said to Joseph, "See, I have set you over all the land of Egypt."

—Genesis 41:37–41

Even Pharaoh could see that God had always been with Joseph. He saw God's wisdom in him and knew Joseph was the obvious choice. He was the only man with enough wisdom to keep Egypt stable in the midst of famine. Pharaoh didn't need to take a vote or interview people to see if someone else was more qualified for the job. God promoted Joseph. It was God's timing. No one rebutted or refused; they all knew Joseph was their man. He would be the one to save the nation.

While reading Joseph's story, we may think just five or ten years passed from the day he received the vision to the day he saw it fulfilled. His story only takes a few chapters. We so often forget to look at the details, the little clues God gives us. Remember, he was seventeen years old when he received the vision (Genesis 37:2), but then: *"Now Joseph was thirty years old when he stood before Pharaoh, king of Egypt"* (Genesis 41:46). Thirteen years had gone by!

Was this the fulfillment of his vision, though? It wasn't the complete fulfillment, but he was now in a position for the dream to come to pass. Joseph was in such a high position of authority that people bowed down and paid homage to him, second-in-command to the king.

When God calls us to a place of honour, it doesn't necessarily mean we'll be in charge. God often needs people to be second-in-command or in different areas of leadership. Joseph didn't have the highest authority, but he was able to influence

Hardships Come to Make Us Stronger

the highest authority. He was in the position God wanted and didn't have to fight for something higher. He was able to be content with the authority given to him.

We need to learn this today. Too often, Christians fight and get jealous of those who are in higher positions or have a greater anointing. They get frustrated instead of being happy with the authority God has given them. Let's be content where God has placed us.

Even though Joseph was in this position of authority, it wasn't time for the full dream to come to pass. First, we need to think about the seven years of plenty that had to pass before his brothers came from Canaan to seek Pharaoh's help. They had to be desperate enough to seek help from the Egyptians. When seven years of plenty had passed, they sought Pharaoh for help.

From the day Joseph had his God-given dream to the day it was fulfilled was at least twenty years. Will you hold on to God's dream for your life for twenty years? You need to hold on, because if God has called you, He will make sure His plans and purposes come to pass.

> *Now Joseph was the ruler over the land; he was the one who sold to all the people of the land. And Joseph's brothers came and bowed down to him with their faces to the ground.*
> —Genesis 42:6

This is where we see Joseph's vision fulfilled. If he had been the same seventeen-year-old boy who'd had this dream, he would have been happy here. This would have been enough. God had been working in him these twenty years, however, so Joseph was different. Through twenty years of hardships, God moulded him. He now understood that the vision wasn't just so his brothers would bow down to him; it served a bigger purpose. God had something greater in mind than just putting Joseph in a high position to exalt Joseph. God wanted to be exalted, so God placed him to make a difference in the world by saving many lives.

Because God worked on Joseph's heart, he was able to see and do things differently. He wasn't doing things for selfish reasons anymore. His goal was no longer to see his brothers bow down to him. Now he wanted to save the very people who had betrayed him. He waited a while and made a plan to get his family to him so he could assist them.

As we continue to read, we see that Joseph is no longer the same. He saw things differently. He didn't want to brag to his brothers or be angry with them for what they had done. He decided to show godly forgiveness. He says in Genesis 45:5, *"Now do not be grieved or angry with yourselves, because you sold me here, for God sent me here to preserve life."* Joseph knew that God had His hand upon him this whole time. Through all his hardships, God was in control. God hadn't left him for a second. The hardships only made him stronger.

Joseph's family was able to move to Egypt where they were saved from the famine that had come to the land. Joseph helped the people who had hurt and betrayed him the most. He didn't wallow in self-pity, but allowed himself to be shaped in the midst of hardship. God made him into a powerful leader.

Let's take a look at what Psalm 105:16–21 says about this story:

> *Moreover He called for a famine in the land; He destroyed all the provision of bread. He sent a man before them—Joseph—who was sold as a slave. They hurt his feet with fetters, He was laid in irons. Until the time that his word came to pass, the word of the Lord tested him. The king*

sent and released him, the ruler of the people let him go free. He made him lord of his house, and ruler of all his possessions... (NKJV)

Here we see that God was in it the whole time. Even in the difficult situations Joseph went through, God was preparing him to be the man He wanted him to become. God was in control from the beginning and in every part in between. God knew when the famine would come, so He prepared Joseph for that time.

We too can be made into powerful men and women of God when we trust God in the midst of difficult circumstances. If God has promised something, He'll definitely bring it to pass. We must look to Joseph's story as an example. What God did for Joseph, He will do for us. We must believe in the midst of our circumstances.

CALLED TO GREATNESS YET WILLING TO SERVE

chapter four

Let's look at someone else in the Bible who was a great success. Throughout the Bible, God calls him a man after His own heart. What a great way to be thought of and remembered, as a person who has a heart to seek God. Since you're reading this book, I believe you have the same desire.

It's always easy to remember the great successes of King David. We like to remember David as the great king and worship leader. Why shouldn't we, since that's the way God remembers him? God doesn't remember our sins and downfalls. Of course, we remember many of his downfalls.

When we first hear about David, he seems to have been rejected and forgotten. The prophet Samuel was in town and God told him to anoint a new king. God gave Samuel instructions, telling him, *"I will send you to Jesse the Bethlehemite, for I have selected a king for Myself among his sons"* (1 Samuel 16:1).

Samuel did as he was commanded and went to visit Jesse. As Samuel saw the oldest sons of Jesse pass by, he thought they were surely God's anointed. They all seemed to be obvious choices. Seven of Jesse's sons had passed, however, and none of them were God's choice. At this point, Samuel must have thought he had missed it. Had he travelled all that way just to find out God hadn't chosen any of Jesse's sons?

Trusting God's Timing

And Samuel said to Jesse, "Are these all the children?"

And [Jesse] said, "There remains yet the youngest, and behold, he is tending the sheep."

Then Samuel said to Jesse, "Send and bring him; for we will not sit down until he comes here."

—1 Samuel 16:11

Can you see how rejected David must have felt? The prophet had come to declare a new king, and it was known to be one of Jesse's sons. David's father called all of his sons (except David) to come and meet the prophet. His father hadn't thought David could possibly be the next king. David had been forgotten; he was the least expected to be anointed king.

It's one thing to not be picked for the soccer team, but to think that one wouldn't even have the chance to be picked? We've all felt bad when we didn't make the team, but how devastating it must have been for David that his own father didn't think to call him.

David was out doing his job, his daily routine. He wasn't waiting for this great calling. He was just happy to be out tending the sheep, being obedient where he was. He wasn't anxious to be somewhere else. He was content out in the field worshipping God.

However, this was the day when David's life suddenly changed. He was no longer going to just be a shepherd boy; he was going to be anointed king. What a change! In the field, he only had sheep under his watch, but now he was going to be expected to care for a whole nation. Not just any nation, but God's nation, His special people.

The Bible doesn't say exactly how old David was. However, many scholars believe he was somewhere between sixteen and eighteen years old. He was just a young man with God's call upon his life. What a great feeling it must have been

Called to Greatness Yet Willing to Serve

to be anointed king in front of his family. It must have seemed strange for them. David hadn't been trained to be a king.

So he sent and brought him in. Now he was ruddy, with beautiful eyes and a handsome appearance. And the Lord said, "Arise, anoint him; for this is he." Then Samuel took the horn of oil and anointed him in the midst of his brothers; and the Spirit of the Lord came mightily upon David from that day forward. And Samuel arose and went to Ramah.
—1 Samuel 16:12–13

As we look a little deeper into David's story, we realize that although he was anointed king, he wasn't yet walking in the fullness of kingship. David was called and God had anointed him, but he still had a lot of preparation to do.

How many people would get frustrated at this point? They've been called. The prophet has given them a word that they will serve the Lord in mighty ways, but for the first couple of years no one even recognizes who they are. Many would become discouraged and think God hadn't spoken to them after all.

We need to realize that just because the word of the Lord has come to us, that doesn't mean it will be accomplished tomorrow or even in the next year. It's for a time to come. Don't get discouraged and think God has to move when you think it's time. God will move when it's His perfect timing, when you're ready.

David received God's calling. He was to be the next man for the job, but he wasn't ready yet. He still had a lot to learn to handle the promotion. He still had a few psalms to write before he could walk in the fullness of his calling. The anointing wasn't enough to sustain him; God had to build his character as well.

Trusting God's Timing

This is what we need to learn. We can be anointed and have a great calling on our lives, but God wants our character to be strong. If we aren't strong in character and integrity, we won't last very long in our anointing. God wants us to be able to withstand the pressures of ministry, and in order to do that we must have a good strong character. God wants His people to arise when they're ready to walk in His calling and not before. If we start before our time, we'll likely face difficulties we aren't equipped to handle.

As David's story develops, God brings him into his calling. I'm sure David could see it too, and he was allowing God to prepare him before he stepped up. David didn't go around proclaiming he was the new king. He kept silent. When God's anointing is upon you, you don't need to announce it. Others will see it and notice you.

After Samuel anointed David, the next thing we see is the current king, Saul, beginning to have problems. At one point he had been God's anointed, but things had changed due to his disobedience. Now that God had anointed someone else, things weren't going so well for Saul.

Now the Spirit of the Lord departed from Saul, and an evil spirit from the Lord terrorized him.
—1 Samuel 16:14

Saul had an evil spirit that was terrorizing him and he was desperate to find relief. Some of the king's servants began to recommend that he seek *"a skillful player of the harp"* (1 Samuel 16:16) to help him. Saul liked the idea, so his servants found him the right person for the job. David's anointing was about to make room for him.

Called to Greatness Yet Willing to Serve

So Saul said to his servants, "Provide for me now a man who can play well and bring him to me."

Then one of the young men said, "Behold, I have seen a son of Jesse the Bethlehemite who is a skillful musician, a mighty man of valor, a warrior, one prudent in speech, and a handsome man; and the Lord is with him."

So Saul sent messengers to Jesse and said, "Send me your son David who is with the flock."

—1 Samuel 16:17–19

Up to this point, it must have seemed far-fetched that David would one day serve the king, let alone be the king. His father didn't even believe it. Here was David, a lonely shepherd boy who loved to worship God on his harp, and he knew God had something more for him. The throne should have gone to Saul's oldest son, so how was David ever going to get in position to become king?

God will move heaven and earth for you to reach His destiny for your life. He's going to make sure that He does what He has promised. It doesn't matter what you're facing or what the odds are. God wouldn't promise you something that He can't make happen. God will shift the things in your life that need to be shifted in order to see His plans fulfilled in you.

Since David had been faithful worshipping God, his skill on the harp made a way for him. He wouldn't have been called into the palace if it weren't for his talent. Notice that David didn't get in there and say, "Yeah, I'm the new king, Saul. You had better get out of here because God has anointed me." David was humble and accepted the job offer knowing that God was with him and God would promote him in His timing.

Then David came to Saul and attended him; and Saul loved him greatly, and he became his armor bearer. Saul sent to Jesse, saying, "Let David now stand before me, for he has found favor in my sight." So it came about whenever the evil spirit from God came to Saul, David would take the harp and play it with his hand; and Saul would be refreshed and be well, and the evil spirit would depart from him.

—1 Samuel 16:21–23

As David played, the anointing of God fell and Saul felt relief. David had an anointing for music. As he played, demons were cast out.

Saul didn't think that one day David would take his throne. David seemed happy just serving Saul. He didn't try to push his way to the top. He placed his confidence in God, knowing that God would do what He'd said He was going to do.

Trouble began to arise in Israel. We all know the story of the giant, Goliath, who came out against the armies of Israel. The armies of Israel were too scared to fight Goliath. David had two jobs at this point—shepherding and playing for Saul—but the Bible says, *"David went back and forth from Saul to tend his father's flock at Bethlehem"* (1 Samuel 17:15).

David had a lot on his plate. He was serving God in every way and did anything that was asked of him. This is a great quality in someone who's going to be a leader one day. David didn't just leave his father's flock to get sick and die, even though he was a powerful worship leader for the king. He remained faithful with the little things. He made sure that he did all that was required of him, even if it meant holding down more than one job.

One day his father called on him to look after his brothers and make sure they were okay. Jesse sent David to bring food. David showed his responsibility in that he didn't just leave the flock alone, even though he was asked to go somewhere else. He made sure someone else could fill in for him.

> *So David arose early in the morning and left the flock with a keeper and took the supplies and went as Jesse had commanded him.*
> —1 Samuel 17:20

I'm sure he was more excited about going to the battle lines than staying home with the flock. However, he wanted to make sure all his responsibilities were covered.

This is another good lesson for us. We may want to step out into a new area of ministry, but we have to make sure there's somebody to handle our old position. Too often, people leave a ministry to do something else without training up anyone in their place. Having someone ready to take over when we leave shows great leadership. It proves one is ready to take on the new responsibility.

As David arrived at the battlefront, he began to hear all that was going on. He had probably heard rumours, but he now saw things firsthand. First, he heard the Philistine yelling at them all day, and he saw that the Israelites were scared (1 Samuel 17:23–24). Then he heard something that made his ears perk up:

> *So the men of Israel said, "Have you seen this man who has come up? Surely he has come up to defy Israel; and it shall be that the man who kills him the king will enrich with great riches, will give him his daughter, and give his father's house exemption from taxes in Israel."*
> —1 Samuel 17:25, NKJV

This was like music to David's ears. He was close to the battle and no one was willing to fight this giant even with the great rewards King Saul had offered. The person who could kill the giant was to receive great riches and also marry the princess—and his family wouldn't have to pay taxes. What a deal! Could the king offer anything better?

Since David was a man who sought God, he was ready for anything. He knew God was on his side and He would fight for him. He didn't need to be afraid. He knew who his God was and who he was in His God. That's what happens as you begin to know the God of the Bible. You see that He is who He says He is. You believe that He will do what He says He will do. That's why it's so important that we set our hearts to seek God!

David began to question the army of Israel. He couldn't understand why they were afraid. How could they give up this great offer from the king? He knew God had fought for Israel in the past and that He would do it again. He was sure that anyone who went to fight Goliath would win. Goliath was the fool. He was messing with God's chosen people. How could he be so stupid?

David knew his God was with him, so he had nothing to be afraid of. David said, *"For who is this uncircumcised Philistine, that he should taunt the armies of the living God?"* (1 Samuel 17:26)

David was furious. Why would people under God's covenant be afraid to fight this guy? God had promised to be with them. David knew that. The rest of the Israelites knew it in their heads, but David had it in his heart—he was sure of it.

When we get into praise and worship as a lifestyle, we begin to see God in a way others don't. As we lift God up over our lives, we see that God is bigger than any of our problems or circumstances. Those who don't make it a habit to seek God won't see Him as all-powerful. They'll only see Him as someone they read about, not as someone personal who will do the same for them.

This is why it's so important that we have a personal relationship with God. He must be our one and only desire. When we get to know His presence, we'll see Him in a whole new light. God will no longer seem far off, but a *"friend who sticks closer than a brother"* (Proverbs 18:24).

The more we develop praise and worship as a lifestyle, the bigger and more personal the God of the universe will become to us. Start to develop a passion for praise and worship in your life. It will change the way you see God!

Since David's heart was so full of God's presence, he wasn't afraid of anything. He couldn't comprehend why others were so afraid. David said to Saul, *"Let no man's heart fail on account of him; your servant will go and fight with this Philistine"* (1 Samuel 17:32).

The only person who had the courage to fight was David. Remember, David was just a youth serving in the king's court, even though he had already been anointed king. He wasn't looking for fame and fortune; he just happened to be the only one with enough courage to fight the giant.

> *Then Saul said to David, "You are not able to go against this Philistine to fight with him; for you are but a youth while he has been a warrior from his youth."*
>
> *But David said to Saul, "Your servant was tending his father's sheep. When a lion or a bear came and took a lamb from the flock, I went out after him and attacked him, and rescued it from his mouth; and when he rose up against me, I seized him by his beard and struck him and killed him. Your servant has killed both the lion and the bear; and this uncircumcised Philistine will be like one of them, since he has taunted the armies of the living God." And David said,*

Trusting God's Timing

"The Lord who delivered me from the paw of the lion and from the paw of the bear, He will deliver me from the hand of this Philistine."

And Saul said to David, "Go, and may the Lord be with you."

—1 Samuel 17:33–37

If we seek fame and fortune, we're seeking the wrong thing. Our main desire needs to be glorifying God. A fulfilled promise should ultimately bring glory to Jesus, not you. When fame is your goal, you lose sight of what's important.

Saul was amazed at David's courage, although he thought the boy was in way over his head. David wasn't afraid to fight while the rest of the army had been paralyzed with fear for over a month. David knew that the circumstances he had faced in the past were preparing him for his future. It wasn't just by chance that he had fought a lion and a bear (1 Samuel 17:34–37). He'd done it because God was preparing him for something bigger. David knew that the battles he'd fought had prepared him to fight the Philistine. If God had given him impossible victories before, He would definitely give him this victory as well.

Despite the horrific things you may have gone through, God has a plan for your future. You may have had the worst life imaginable, yet God will use it for something great. It could be to help someone who's going through the same thing, or maybe you could share your testimony about how God helped you survive and forgive the people who harmed you. God doesn't put you through these things. He didn't want the bad things to happen in your life, but He can use them for His glory. So many people have powerful testimonies, but they're too afraid or ashamed to share them. Many people could be set free if they would just share what they've been through. You never

Called to Greatness Yet Willing to Serve

know who might be listening. Others may have faced similar situations in their lives and need to hear how God helped you.

David appeared to be the least qualified for the job, like when he was chosen to be king. He wouldn't have been the people's choice to go and fight. As we look for leaders, we must look for the one that God's choosing, not just the one who wants the position and looks like they have great potential.

In this story, David was the only one who was willing. No one else had the courage to fight the giant. David gave his qualifications. He had killed a bear and a lion. God had delivered those animals into his hand, so He was going to do the same with this uncircumcised Philistine. David had courage because God had fought for him in the past.

Once Saul saw that David was the only person willing to fight the giant, he sent him out: *"Go, and may the Lord be with you"* (1 Samuel 17:37). He noticed that David was determined. David was excited and passionate, and nothing was going to turn him away. He was going to show the rest of the world how great God is—and he wasn't going to do it the traditional way with armour and a sword.

> *He took his stick in his hand and chose for himself five smooth stones from the brook, and put them in the shepherd's bag which he had, even in his pouch, and his sling was in his hand; and he approached the Philistine.*
> —1 Samuel 17:40

In the natural, this seems crazy. How was David going to defeat a world-renowned champion fighter with a stick, a few small stones, and a sling? He was going in without physical protection. He had no armour, but He had his God and he knew that was enough. He didn't need anything else.

When Goliath looked at David, he couldn't believe his eyes. The rest of the army stood back, hiding, and the only one willing to challenge him was a youth? He must have been laughing on the inside. He said, *"Am I a dog, that you come to me with sticks?' And the Philistine cursed David by his gods"* (1 Samuel 17:43). He must have thought Saul was kidding him. Why was the king of Israel sending out a youth to fight his battles? Goliath was sure he was going to win this one. What Goliath didn't know was that God had been preparing David to be the next king. God's hand was upon him.

David had confidence knowing that God had anointed him. God had already told him that one day he was going to be king. At this point, he was only one of many servants, but the fact that God had anointed him was enough for David to fight someone bigger and more experienced than him. He knew that if God had promised him kingship, God would fight for him. God would bring about the victory.

This is why we can't let hard challenges hold us back. If God has called us, He will give us supernatural strength. He'll open doors only He can open.

We need to learn to trust God as David did. He may have seemed far from what he was called to do, but he knew his calling would come to pass one day in God's timetable. If we get too discouraged in the challenge, we'll break. We must always remember the day when God called us, the day when the anointing came upon us. This will give us strength and courage to move on.

I give this advice to young couples planning to marry. I said this to my wife before we got married. I said, "Karla, do you remember the day when God spoke to you, when God told you to marry me?" When she said yes to that, I added, "Okay, always remember that day. When hard circumstances and difficulties come in our marriage, we will always remember that

God spoke to us, and because He spoke to us, we will make it through." If He didn't speak to us, we'll become discouraged and want to give up. People get divorced because they forget that God spoke to them to marry that person. God doesn't change His mind.

Before you do anything, be sure that you have a word from God. Be sure you have heard Him speak. Once you have that assurance, nothing will stop you. You'll be able to face the hardest circumstances and persecution because you know that you know that you know that God is on your side. God spoke, so it will happen. He will accomplish what He has spoken to you. It's so important that we have a word from God.

We can hear the confidence in David's response to the Philistine:

You come to me with a sword, a spear, and a javelin, but I come to you in the name of the Lord of hosts, the God of the armies of Israel, whom you have taunted. This day the Lord will deliver you up into my hands, and I will strike you down and remove your head from you. And I will give the dead bodies of the army of the Philistines this day to the birds of the sky and the wild beasts of the earth, that all the earth may know that there is a God in Israel, and that all this assembly may know that the Lord does not deliver by sword or by spear; for the battle is the Lord's and He will give you into our hands.

—1 Samuel 17:45–47

You see, David knew in his heart that God was going to bring about the victory. David wasn't coming to fight the Philistine by himself. He had God behind him. That's why he could trash-talk the giant: "I am going to cut your head off and feed the rest of your dead body to the birds." David's strength came from knowing God was with him. That's where we need to find our strength. You must know that God's with you.

You've probably already heard the end of this story. You know what's going to happen, but let's read it again and remember that we can apply these stories to our own lives. We may not be fighting giants in the physical realm, but we'll face them in the spiritual realm.

> *Then it happened when the Philistine rose and came and drew near to meet David, that David ran quickly toward the battle line to meet the Philistine. And David put his hand into his bag and took from it a stone and slung it, and struck the Philistine on his forehead. And the stone sank into his forehead, so that he fell on his face to the ground.*
>
> *Thus David prevailed over the Philistine with a sling and a stone, and he struck the Philistine and killed him; but there was no sword in David's hand. Then David ran and stood over the Philistine and took his sword and drew it out of its sheath and killed him, and cut off his head with it. When the Philistines saw that their champion was dead, they fled.*
>
> —1 Samuel 17:48–51

What a victory God brought forth! David wouldn't have been able to kill this giant on his own, but because God was with him, he could. Not only was God with him, he knew God was with him. There's a difference. We need to know that God's with us *and* that He's fighting for us.

This is a good time to remember that this victory happened before David became king. He knew that one day he would be king because God had anointed him for that, but he wasn't just sitting around waiting for it to happen. He saw an opportunity for God to move and wanted to be a part of it. He wasn't stepping on anybody to get to the top. He knew that anyone could have fought this giant and won, but he was the only one willing to do so.

Don't use and manipulate others to try to get to where God has called you. That's walking according to the flesh and we're called to walk by the Spirit. Be confident, knowing you will get there in His timing. You don't need to rush. When God has placed His vision inside of you, it's for a set time, maybe years down the road. God shows us the potential we have when we walk with Him.

We need to be secure in our calling. When someone is insecure, you can see it. They push and try to make things happen. When you trust in the God who called you, you know there's a process, and you won't get there until you're ready. You can't skip steps to get to your calling. The best way to go is God's way. Be willing to wait for the vision to come to pass. When you're ready, you'll be glad you waited.

Every victory for David brought him closer to what God had anointed him for. When he had the opportunity to serve the king, that was a victory. He was humble enough to know that one day he would take the king's place, but he didn't brag about it or get puffed up. When he defeated Goliath, the experience prepared him to be the man of war he would become as king. David lived one day at a time, confident in his call. He didn't need it to happen quickly; he knew it was going to happen in God's timing.

THE IMPORTANCE OF FRIENDSHIPS

chapter five

David had another great thing going for him: he understood the importance of friendships. We need to have close friendships. God has developed us this way. The friendship between David and Jonathan is very touching.

Think of this. Jonathan was Saul's firstborn son, born to inherit his father's throne. It would be easy for one to be jealous of the other. David could have been jealous knowing that the throne legally belonged to Jonathan, and Jonathan could have been jealous knowing David had been elected by God to sit on the throne. Yet these two became close friends.

> *Now it came about when he had finished speaking to Saul, that the soul of Jonathan was knit to the soul of David, and Jonathan loved him as himself. Saul took him that day and did not let him return to his father's house. Then Jonathan made a covenant with David because he loved him as himself. Jonathan stripped himself of the robe that was on him and gave it to David, with his armor, including his sword and his bow and his belt.*
> —1 Samuel 18:1–4

Jonathan and David became such good friends that they made a covenant to protect one another. When King Saul saw that David and Jonathan were good friends, he decided to bring David into the palace. He no longer let him go back to his father's house. He wasn't a shepherd anymore. God had taken him out of that place and lined him up for what He had for him next.

We need to understand the seasons of God. There's a time for us to stay where we are, even though we may not enjoy it, knowing God has something greater for us. At one point, David was called to be a shepherd, and he stayed there even after he was anointed king. He knew it wasn't time to leave his position in his father's house. Many times we don't enjoy the job we're in. We want to do more, but God has us there for a reason, and it's important that we stay and be faithful there for a season.

Friendships in the kingdom of God are vital. We all need people who are close to us and can speak into our lives. We need people we can trust, people who we can laugh and talk with and let loose and have a good time. This is how we strengthen one another.

As we'll see later on, Jonathan often protected David. Jonathan was going to make sure David walked in his calling, even if it meant him losing his inheritance. Jonathan wanted what God wanted.

Up to this point, everything was going great for David. He was in the palace serving the king. Whenever he was asked to do something, he did it. He was very obedient to whatever the king ordered (1 Samuel 18:5). The people also loved David. I'm sure David was happy and had nothing to worry about. So far, he was moving closer to the throne without any opposition. Saul loved him and Jonathan was his best friend who was willing to give him the kingdom.

The Importance of Friendships

It only took one event for this to change, and for David's confidence to be tried. A couple of ladies drastically changed David's life. King Saul was to be filled with so much jealousy and hatred that he would persecute David for the rest of his life.

It happened as they were coming, when David returned from killing the Philistine, that the women came out of all the cities of Israel, singing and dancing, to meet King Saul, with tambourines, with joy and with musical instruments. The women sang as they played, and said, "Saul has slain his thousands, and David his ten thousands."

Then Saul became very angry, for this saying displeased him; and he said, "They have ascribed to David ten thousands, but to me they have ascribed thousands. Now what more can he have but the kingdom?" Saul looked at David with suspicion from that day on.

—1 Samuel 18:6–9

How could things change so fast for David? He was doing God's will and was obedient to the king. The moment others began to praise him, Saul was gripped with jealousy. For a time, King Saul had seemed fine—the evil spirit hadn't been bothering him—but he opened a door for oppression again the day he gave in to jealousy.

This is an easy trap for us to fall into. We can lose sight that we're each given a calling. Jealousy can come to all of us. This often happens when we see others doing better or being used in more prominent ways than we are. It's sometimes harder when we see another's faults and wonder why God would use that person. We need to die to our jealousy and allow God to work in us. If we allow jealousy to fester, it will erupt quickly, just like it did in Saul.

Trusting God's Timing

Now it came about on the next day that an evil spirit from God came mightily upon Saul, and he raved in the midst of the house, while David was playing the harp with his hand, as usual; and a spear was in Saul's hand. Saul hurled the spear for he thought, "I will pin David to the wall." But David escaped from his presence twice.

—1 Samuel 18:10–11

The jealousy in Saul's heart became so great that he was even willing to kill David, his faithful servant and his son's best friend. Even though David had been the one God used to bring Saul relief, the king could no longer receive relief because of his jealousy.

Once a door is opened, it can't be shut until there is true repentance. We can't expect to hold jealousy or other sins in our hearts and continue on in the joy of the Lord. The joy will vanish as we magnify the offenses we've allowed in our hearts. In Saul's case, it was the fact that David had a greater victory than he ever had. David had defeated Goliath and made the Philistine army flee before the army of Israel. What had Saul done during his reign?

Now Saul was afraid of David, for the Lord was with him but had departed from Saul. Therefore Saul removed him from his presence and appointed him as his commander of a thousand; and he went out and came in before the people. David was prospering in all his ways for the Lord was with him. When Saul saw that he was prospering greatly, he dreaded him. But all Israel and Judah loved David, and he went out and came in before them.

—1 Samuel 18:12–16

The Importance of Friendships

Saul could no longer work with David since the people were recognizing David's leadership skills. If Saul had been a godly leader, he would have seen these skills in David. Instead of getting jealous, he would have helped him to grow stronger in his gifting. But Saul could see that God was with David, and that made him afraid of losing his position and the love of the people. He thought he needed to get rid of David and the threat to his throne. He wasn't willing to give up control and make way for the new king God was preparing.

From this point, David went through years of persecution. I believe the only things that kept him going was his friendship with Jonathan and the knowledge that God had called him. Despite all the persecution, he knew he would one day be the king he'd been anointed to be. God was going to protect him and make sure he made it to the throne.

Let's go back to the importance of David's friendship with Jonathan. When the persecution got tough, it was Jonathan who helped David escape. Jonathan and David wanted the best for one another. This was the strong foundation of their relationship. They were willing to put their lives on the line for each other.

David knew Saul wanted to kill him. He'd already had a few spears thrown at him by Saul, and that was enough to make him want to run. Jonathan was willing to stand in the gap for his friend and protect him. Jonathan made sure David was all right and helped him reach God's best, even when it meant Jonathan losing his rightful position.

"If it please my father to do you harm, may the Lord do so to Jonathan and more also, if I do not make it known to you and send you away, that you may go in safety. And may the Lord be with you as He has been with my father. If I am still alive, will you not show me the lovingkindness of the Lord,

> *that I may not die? You shall not cut off your lovingkindness from my house forever, not even when the Lord cuts off every one of the enemies of David from the face of the earth." So Jonathan made a covenant with the house of David, saying, "May the Lord require it at the hands of David's enemies." Jonathan made David vow again because of his love for him, because he loved him as he loved his own life.*
>
> —1 Samuel 20:13–17

Jonathan knew his father was going to be very angry with him, yet their friendship meant more to him than fear for his own life. At this point, Jonathan decided to make a covenant with David, a pact so strong that it was to last for generations.

Once David and Jonathan made a plan to find out about King Saul's plans for David, they departed. Jonathan covered for David. True friendships will always protect one another. Jonathan was willing to protect David even from the king of the land. It didn't take Jonathan long to figure out that David was right and Saul indeed wanted to kill him. The jealousy in Saul's heart was apparent to everyone. Saul knew how close his son and David were, but he couldn't hide his hatred from his own son. Jonathan was so loyal to David that he stood up for him against his father.

> *Then Saul's anger burned against Jonathan and he said to him, "You son of a perverse, rebellious woman! Do I not know that you are choosing the son of Jesse to your own shame and to the shame of your mother's nakedness? For as long as the son of Jesse lives on the earth, neither you nor your kingdom will be established. Therefore now, send and bring him to me, for he must surely die."*
>
> —1 Samuel 20:30–31

The Importance of Friendships

Saul was proud, and that's why he couldn't see what his son saw. Saul tried to remind Jonathan that he wouldn't be king if David took the throne. Jonathan had already humbly accepted that David would take the throne, because that was God's will. Neither he nor Saul could do anything to stop it.

Jonathan had David's back. Listen to Jonathan's response to his father.

> *But Jonathan answered Saul his father and said to him, "Why should he be put to death? What has he done?" Then Saul hurled his spear at him to strike him down; so Jonathan knew that his father had decided to put David to death. Then Jonathan arose from the table in fierce anger, and did not eat food on the second day of the new moon, for he was grieved over David because his father had dishonored him.*
> —1 Samuel 20:32–34

When Jonathan confronted his father's jealousy, it almost got him killed. Jonathan knew David's heart and that he didn't want him to die. Although David was called to be king, he would never harm Saul or Jonathan. A true friend will know your heart and every intention. Sincerity makes a friendship true. Jonathan knew he had to warn David about his father. He couldn't deny it any longer if he wanted to protect his best friend.

Although this persecution caused David to flee for his life, he still loved and cared for Jonathan. Their friendship remained strong. Distance and time separated David and Jonathan, but their love and friendship for one another never wavered.

We can see this because there were times when Saul was looking for David and Jonathan came to meet David and encourage him (1 Samuel 23:15–18). Even though they had been separated, they couldn't be torn apart. They wouldn't forget about one another.

We all need a Jonathan in our lives. Too many Lone Rangers have lost sight of the call of God. We need friends who encourage us in tough situations and help us become stronger in God.

SEEKING GOD: THE KEY TO SUCCESS

chapter six

Sometimes we look at David's story and forget about all the struggles he had to go through before becoming king. Many of us today want to be pastors and leaders, but we don't want to pay the price they had to pay. When we're sure in our calling, we're willing to wait and allow God to prepare us.

When people doubt or are unsure, they take shortcuts to be able to get where they think God's calling them. God may allow them to walk in that position, but with nowhere near the ability and anointing He wants them to move in. God can only bring us to the next level when we're willing to allow Him to work in us completely and understand that persecutions aren't there to break or intimidate us. We must rise above the persecutions that come against us and stand strong in the calling God has given us.

Saul persecuted David for close to fifteen years. David had been called to be king as a young boy, but he wasn't ready for what he would face as king until he had matured. Throughout the rest of 1 Samuel, we see David running for his life, hiding from Saul. In the natural, the calling he'd received probably seemed like a distant dream, one that would never happen, but God always has a way to accomplish His plan for us.

Although David was driven into the wilderness, and his whole family had to flee their homeland, instead of getting bitter and angry with God he decided to see the best in every situation. When David escaped from Saul, he encountered men with potential, people God could use for His glory. However, only a true leader could see the potential in these people.

So David departed from there and escaped to the cave of Adullam; and when his brothers and all his father's household heard of it, they went down there to him. Everyone who was in distress, and everyone who was in debt, and everyone who was discontented gathered to him; and he became captain over them. Now there were about four hundred men with him.
—1 Samuel 22:1–2

David may have wanted to give himself a pity party. Maybe he wanted to complain about being chased and that God had abandoned him. Instead he began to train leaders. Everyone who was troubled began to be drawn to him. He spoke to their potential, and soon these men would be his mighty army.

Many people around us started out as alcoholics, drug addicts, and prostitutes, but God has a great redemptive plan for them. As they are healed and restored, God's going to use them to bring healing and restoration to others.

In the middle of his difficult circumstances, David decided to continue being faithful to God. He was going to be the leader he'd been called to be and continue preparing himself for the calling God had given him, even if it seemed impossible. Often people crumble and fall when they're in these types of circumstances. I hope this book encourages you to break through intimidation and realize your potential. God has called you to something and He's preparing you for it no matter how difficult your life may look right now.

Seeking God: The Key to Success

Don't get me wrong. I'm not saying everyone has to go through persecution in order to receive God's best. God works with people in a variety of ways. Abraham didn't have to go through persecution that we know of; God needed to deal with Abraham in other areas. Each of us has a unique calling. God will lead us into it using different scenarios. Persecution can help us when we understand that it builds our character. Notice that David didn't break under the pressure.

As the old Elbert Hubbard saying goes, "When life gives you lemons, make lemonade." Make something out of the persecutions you're going through. Don't look at them as obstacles; see them as a launching pad for God to bring you to the next level.

Saul, on the other hand, made so many mistakes. God had already decided he was no longer fit to be king (1 Samuel 15:23). God spoke very clearly. How was Saul going to hold on to what God had already told him he was going to lose?

If Saul had been humble, he would have understood that he had failed and God was giving his position to another. The problem is he wasn't humble. Saul was so prideful, he thought that if he killed David, he could keep the kingship in his family. He figured he could keep God from taking the kingdom away from him.

Saul opened himself up to pride and jealousy and began to do things he wouldn't have if he didn't have rebellion in his heart. In contrast, David was humble and confident in God. He knew that if God anointed him, he would one day be king no matter how many times Saul tried to kill him. He knew God's hand of protection was on him. He had nothing to be afraid of. He didn't have to fight back. God was with him.

Once God has promised you something, you can be assured it will come to pass. You can know that God will turn

Trusting God's Timing

terrible circumstances around to your favour. God always has a plan, no matter how lost you think you are.

David was a man of worship and prayer, and he knew that he should seek the face of God before he did anything. How many difficult circumstances could we avoid if we would learn from his example? While David was in the midst of persecution and Saul's army was hunting him, he still took the time to seek God. He wasn't afraid, but he didn't want to walk outside of God's will. He wanted to be sure that he was doing what God had called him to do.

Look at what David says:

Though a host encamp against me, my heart will not fear; though war arise against me, in spite of this I shall be confident.

—Psalm 27:3

David knew God was with him, so he had no need to fear. God was on his side. What more could David ask for? God's always fighting for you.

I'm sure there were many times when all David wanted to do was give up and go back to shepherding sheep. He hadn't planned to live on the run. The day he'd been anointed, he hadn't thought he would go through fifteen years of persecution before walking in the calling.

David wanted to be sure that he didn't do anything outside of God's will for his life. So when he heard that *"the Philistines are fighting against Keilah and are plundering the threshing floors"* (1 Samuel 23:1), he paused to seek the Lord before he acted.

So David inquired of the Lord, saying, "Shall I go and attack these Philistines?"

Seeking God: The Key to Success

And the Lord said to David, "Go and attack the Philistines and deliver Keilah."

But David's men said to him, "Behold, we are afraid here in Judah. How much more then if we go to Keilah against the ranks of the Philistines?"

Then David inquired of the Lord once more. And the Lord answered him and said, "Arise, go down to Keilah, for I will give the Philistines into your hand."

So David and his men went to Keilah and fought with the Philistines; and he led away their livestock and struck them with a great slaughter. Thus David delivered the inhabitants of Keilah.

—1 Samuel 23:2–5

Even though David knew God could help him succeed over the Philistines, he still sought God. He wanted to make sure it was the right timing. God had already promised to give his enemies into his hand, but he didn't want to do something just for the sake of doing it.

David had a word from God, but his people were afraid. He didn't want to bring people with him who weren't sure God would be with them. Despite having a word for himself, he still asked God for a word for his army. Once they all had a word, he went in to attack.

It was important for him to seek God first, and now we'll see why.

When it was told Saul that David had come to Keilah, Saul said, "God has delivered him into my hand, for he shut himself in by entering a city with double gates and bars." So Saul summoned all the people for war, to go down to Keilah to besiege David and his men.

—1 Samuel 23:7–8

If David hadn't sought God first, he wouldn't have been ready for this news. If he had just assumed God was with him, he may have been surprised and terrified once he heard about Saul. However, he knew God would protect him. God wouldn't have told him to go down to Keilah if He didn't have a plan.

Since David had the habit of seeking God, when this news came, he wasn't shaken. He did the same thing he always did: he asked God what he should do next.

> *Then David said, "O Lord God of Israel, Your servant has heard for certain that Saul is seeking to come to Keilah to destroy the city on my account. Will the men of Keilah surrender me into his hand? Will Saul come down just as Your servant has heard? O Lord God of Israel, I pray, tell Your servant." And the Lord said, "He will come down." Then David said, "Will the men of Keilah surrender me and my men into the hand of Saul?" And the Lord said, "They will surrender you."*
>
> —1 Samuel 23:10–12

David made sure his allies were loyal to him. He couldn't trust the men of Keilah to take care of him even after he'd helped them with their enemies. One would have expected them to help, but he wasn't willing to take the chance without seeking God's input. Most of us would have assumed that the men of Keilah owed us one for saving them from their enemies. We wouldn't have even thought to seek God for this. Others would have asked Keilah for help instead of seeking refuge in God.

It's a good thing for David that he loved to seek God. As he sought God, God was able to assure him that the men of Keilah would deliver him into King Saul's hands. This wasn't good news, but David needed to hear it. God won't just tell us what we want to hear. He'll be sure to share the truth with us. The truth sometimes hurts and brings confusion, but God always brings clarity, *"[f]or God is not the author of confusion but of peace"* (1 Corinthians 14:33, NKJV).

Because David knew about the betrayal of the men of Keilah, he knew he had to leave and find safe refuge. Thankfully, David was able to escape. God helped him get away with about six hundred of his men, and Saul gave up the pursuit (1 Samuel 23:13).

Now David was forced to go into hiding in caves. If he left those caves, he probably would have been killed. I'm sure David had lots of time to seek God while in hiding. God even sent someone to encourage him, the person he wanted to see more than anyone else: his best friend, Jonathan.

Now David became aware that Saul had come out to seek his life while David was in the wilderness of Ziph at Horesh. And Jonathan, Saul's son, arose and went to David at Horesh, and encouraged him in God. Thus he said to him, "Do not be afraid, because the hand of Saul my father will not find you, and you will be king over Israel and I will be next to you; and Saul my father knows that also." So the two of them made a covenant before the Lord; and David stayed at Horesh while Jonathan went to his house.
—1 Samuel 23:15–18

God will send the right people to speak to us when we need it most. As we seek God's face, He'll be sure to speak to us, sometimes directly and other times through people we respect. The key is to seek God's face continually.

After hearing Jonathan's word of encouragement, people again began to betray David by telling Saul where he was hiding. God allowed David to escape through faithful friends who advised him when Saul knew his location.

> *When Saul and his men went to seek him, they told David, and he came down to the rock and stayed in the wilderness of Maon. And when Saul heard it, he pursued David in the wilderness of Maon. Saul went on one side of the mountain, and David and his men on the other side of the mountain; and David was hurrying to get away from Saul, for Saul and his men were surrounding David and his men to seize them. But a messenger came to Saul, saying, "Hurry and come, for the Philistines have made a raid on the land." So Saul returned from pursuing David and went to meet the Philistines; therefore they called that place the Rock of Escape. David went up from there and stayed in the strongholds of Engedi.*
> —1 Samuel 23:25–29

Since David sought God's heart continually, God protected him. When everything looked like death and destruction, God distracted Saul so that he could escape.

When you know that God has called you, you can go through persecution and hard times because God will do the impossible for you. He will always make a way for His anointed. David was able to rest assured that he was in God's will. He saw time and again how God protected him and supernaturally delivered him from King Saul's hand. When things looked rough, David didn't even flinch—and neither should you.

GOD'S WAY, NOT YOUR WAY

chapter seven

When God calls us, we can be tempted into taking shortcuts to the place where God has called us. Even Jesus was tempted by Satan to take the easier route (Matthew 4:8–9). When going through trials, hardships, and persecutions, we must keep our eyes on Jesus and remember that when Jesus is Lord of our lives, He'll make sure we get to the place of anointing.

The truth is that we don't like to wait. It isn't in our DNA to patiently wait for the promised outcome. We want to get there as fast as we can and look for the quickest way. If we want to fulfill our destiny, we must learn to do things God's way and in His timing. We can never rush ahead of Him.

The best results for our lives will come when we submit to God's plans. As we realize that He has our best intentions in mind, we can be focused and sure that He will do what's best for us.

Difficult circumstances aren't made to break us. They should actually make us stronger. We need to remember this as we go through trials. God has designed us to rise above our circumstances and be all He has called us to be.

Trusting God's Timing

Consider it all joy, my brethren, when you encounter various trials, knowing that the testing of your faith produces endurance. And let endurance have its perfect result, so that you may be perfect and complete, lacking in nothing.

—James 1:2–4

Hard times shouldn't cause us to quit. We should decide to learn all we can from difficult times. As we learn, we become better equipped for our assignment. God doesn't send the trials, but He uses them to mould us into His image. If we want to be like Him, we must go through our difficulties like Jesus went through His (Hebrews 5:8–9).

While David was in the midst of difficult circumstances, he had a chance to deliver himself from them. The problem is that it would have been his way, not God's way. David had this opportunity twice, but he allowed God to be glorified.

David, hiding in the strongholds of Engedi, had been running from place to place until he was seemingly safe. But he knew Saul would find him eventually. He couldn't stay there forever.

Now when Saul returned from pursuing the Philistines, he was told, saying, "Behold, David is in the wilderness of Engedi." Then Saul took three thousand chosen men from all Israel and went to seek David and his men in front of the Rocks of the Wild Goats.

—1 Samuel 24:1–2

David only had six hundred men with him. Saul must have been quite afraid of David, since he brought five times that. Saul knew they were mighty men, but even more he knew God was with them. He thought maybe he had a chance to kill David if his army outnumbered them.

God's Way, Not Your Way

Saul looked for David with three thousand men. They searched everywhere until Saul had to stop in a cave, having to go to the bathroom. He didn't realize that this cave was the very place where David would have a chance to kill him. If you don't believe me, keep reading.

He came to the sheepfolds on the way, where there was a cave; and Saul went in to relieve himself. Now David and his men were sitting in the inner recesses of the cave. The men of David said to him, "Behold, this is the day of which the Lord said to you, 'Behold, I am about to give your enemy into your hand, and you shall do to him as it seems good to you.'"

Then David arose and cut off the edge of Saul's robe secretly. It came about afterward that David's conscience bothered him because he had cut off the edge of Saul's robe. So he said to his men, "Far be it from me because of the Lord that I should do this thing to my lord, the Lord's anointed, to stretch out my hand against him, since he is the Lord's anointed." David persuaded his men with these words and did not allow them to rise up against Saul. And Saul arose, left the cave, and went on his way.

—1 Samuel 24:3–7

David's men thought it would be a good idea to kill Saul. They said God had given David's enemies into his hand. Their reasoning seemed good, but it was a cover for seeking revenge. Our way of doing things is taking justice into our own hands, but that isn't God's way.

Even though killing Saul would have been a quick solution to David's problems, he wasn't going to sin against God to get there. He knew God would put him on the throne when He wanted him to sit on the throne.

Trusting God's Timing

David was confident in his calling. He recalled the time when the prophet Samuel had come to his home and anointed him king. He'd known he wasn't ready at the time, but God was preparing him to be the king of Israel. As he submitted to God's will, he knew he would fulfill God's plan for his life.

This kind of confidence in God's call can be hard to find. Many aren't sure if God can really use them. They don't realize that all the great men of God went through a process of growth. No one had it together the day they were called. Nobody has woken up the next day after God gave them a vision and saw it fulfilled. God's vision is always for an appointed time, and we must do it God's way, not our way.

We will see David's integrity again. When David gets a second chance to do away with Saul, end his problems, and receive the throne, he didn't take it. He was totally submitted to God's plan for his life. He wasn't going to take any shortcuts to get there.

Once again, someone told Saul where David was hiding (1 Samuel 26:1–3). He could never stay in the same spot for very long. However, David knew that God's hand of protection was on him. He was going to be delivered, one way or another. God's plans would be fulfilled.

So David and Abishai came to the people by night, and behold, Saul lay sleeping inside the circle of the camp with his spear stuck in the ground at his head; and Abner and the people were lying around him. Then Abishai said to David, "Today God has delivered your enemy into your hand; now therefore, please let me strike him with the spear to the ground with one stroke, and I will not strike him the second time." But David said to Abishai, "Do not destroy him, for who can stretch out his hand against the Lord's anointed and be without guilt?" David also said, "As the Lord lives, surely the Lord will strike

God's Way, Not Your Way

him, or his day will come that he dies, or he will go down into battle and perish. The Lord forbid that I should stretch out my hand against the Lord's anointed; but now please take the spear that is at his head and the jug of water, and let us go." So David took the spear and the jug of water from beside Saul's head, and they went away, but no one saw or knew it, nor did any awake, for they were all asleep, because a sound sleep from the Lord had fallen on them.

—1 Samuel 26:7–12

Since David had refused to kill Saul the first time, Abishai thought maybe he could do it for him. Besides, what are friends for? Right? Wrong. David wasn't going to allow someone to help him fulfill God's plan any faster. He knew God was taking care of him. He knew that Saul was going to die and he would be king. He was assured that he didn't have to push to get his way.

David took the spear and jug of water beside Saul's head. This was proof that he'd had a chance to kill Saul but refused to do it. He wanted to prove to Saul that he had integrity and didn't have any malice in his heart, even though Saul wanted him dead. Instead of killing Saul, David told him, once again, that God had given him a chance to kill him but he hadn't taken it.

So David said to Abner, "Are you not a man? And who is like you in Israel? Why then have you not guarded your lord the king? For one of the people came to destroy the king your lord. This thing that you have done is not good. As the Lord lives, all of you must surely die, because you did not guard your lord, the Lord's anointed. And now, see where the king's spear is and the jug of water that was at his head."

—1 Samuel 26:15–16

David called out to Saul's armour bearer to show him that he hadn't protected the king. He wasn't doing his job right—he had fallen asleep. There could have been some terrible consequences for that, one being that the king would have died and so would he.

> *Then Saul recognized David's voice and said, "Is this your voice, my son David?"*
>
> *And David said, "It is my voice, my lord the king." He also said, "Why then is my lord pursuing his servant? For what have I done? Or what evil is in my hand?*
>
> —1 Samuel 26:17–18

David had shown, for the second time, that he wasn't going to do Saul harm. He had made a commitment to do no damage to Saul whatsoever.

If David hadn't done anything deserving of death and didn't seek revenge, why was Saul chasing him? After being confronted for the second time, it appears as though Saul repented from chasing David. He apologized and was grateful that David had spared his life. Listen to what Saul says:

> *I have sinned. Return, my son David, for I will not harm you again because my life was precious in your sight this day. Behold, I have played the fool and have committed a serious error.*
>
> —1 Samuel 26:21

Saul was telling the truth. He didn't pursue David any longer. From that day forward, David was free and didn't have to stay in hiding. Or did he? Could he have trusted Saul?

1 Samuel 27 shows that David wasn't one hundred percent sure he could trust Saul's promise, so he went back into hiding. This time, he decided to hide in his enemy's territory.

> *Now it was told Saul that David had fled to Gath, so he no longer searched for him.*
> —1 Samuel 27:4

Yes, Saul had finally backed off and David didn't need to be afraid anymore. However, this wasn't the end of his troubles. Before becoming king, he would have to face one more.

David hid in Philistine territory for a few years until they no longer wanted him. The Philistines became afraid he might turn on them, as they knew of David's fame.

> *Is this not David, of whom they sing in the dances, saying, "Saul has slain his thousands, and David his ten thousands"?*
> —1 Samuel 29:5

They couldn't trust David enough to fight with them, for they knew he had killed their greatest warrior, Goliath. So they sent David home where he would find more trouble. Instead of peace, he encountered more tribulation.

> *When David and his men came to the city, behold, it was burned with fire, and their wives and their sons and their daughters had been taken captive. Then David and the people who were with him lifted their voices and wept until there was no strength in them to weep. Now David's two wives had been taken captive...*
> —1 Samuel 30:3–5

Trusting God's Timing

David went home on a peaceful afternoon only to find that the entire territory had been raided. He lost everything. This must have been a hard moment for the soon-to-be king. Yet David was a fighter. He wasn't going to give up, and neither should you.

Moreover David was greatly distressed because the people spoke of stoning him, for all the people were embittered, each one because of his sons and his daughters. But David strengthened himself in the Lord his God.
—1 Samuel 30:6

Many people respond to difficult times in a church by blaming a leader and leaving instead of seeking God. Most people who go through disappointments such as this one don't know how to get back up. They believe God has abandoned them and caused the crisis to happen. I have good news for you: it wasn't God who did it; it was the enemy. You need to rise up as David did. He didn't let these mishaps affect his calling. He refused to give up on God! David's response was different from everyone else's because he was sure of God's goodness. The same God who had protected him all these years was going to be his source of strength.

Instead of playing the blame game, find your strength in God's presence. Seek His face. There's no better thing to do than to get in His presence. Don't be afraid to ask God what happened. Give Him your frustrations and disappointments. He wants to turn things around for you. He will always lead you in triumph (2 Corinthians 2:14).

Since David knew to seek God, he knew to ask Him what he was to do next. Remember, he had done this before. It was the only logical thing for him to do.

God's Way, Not Your Way

David inquired of the Lord, saying, "Shall I pursue this band? Shall I overtake them?" And He said to him, "Pursue, for you will surely overtake them, and you will surely rescue all."

—1 Samuel 30:8

The rest had given up and would have killed their leader, probably ending up in a long-term depression. David sought God and got directions to fight because God was going to give him the victory and restore to him all that the enemy had stolen.

Don't give up, no matter how bad things look, because God wants to do the same for you.

David slaughtered them from the twilight until the evening of the next day; and not a man of them escaped, except four hundred young men who rode on camels and fled. So David recovered all that the Amalekites had taken, and rescued his two wives. But nothing of theirs was missing, whether small or great, sons or daughters, spoil or anything that they had taken for themselves; David brought it all back.

—1 Samuel 30:17–19

What a victory! David was able to recover everything the enemy had stolen; God didn't allow him to lose a thing. But if he had listened to everyone else and given in to despair, he would have lost everything.

This was a very important time for David, though he didn't realize it at the time. As he was fighting, a battle was fought between the Israelites and Philistines which ended in King Saul's death. David's defeat could have caused him to quit right before he received his promotion. If he had given up and allowed the people to stone him, he wouldn't have

Trusting God's Timing

accomplished the calling God had given him. He would have died before completing God's call.

How sad that so many great callings go unfulfilled due to a setback. David knew to seek God in every circumstance.

> *So Saul took his sword and fell on it. When his armor bearer saw that Saul was dead, he also fell on his sword and died with him. Thus Saul died with his three sons, his armor bearer, and all his men on that day together.*
> —1 Samuel 31:4–6

Now that Saul was dead, David was set to receive the crown. Everyone knew he had been anointed for the position. After many years of struggle, he was finally about to see the vision of God fulfilled.

> *Then David took hold of his clothes and tore them, and so also did all the men who were with him. They mourned and wept and fasted until evening for Saul and his son Jonathan and for the people of the Lord and the house of Israel, because they had fallen by the sword.*
> —2 Samuel 1:11–12

Notice that David didn't want Saul to die. He hadn't prayed for God to kill him and didn't rejoice when he heard about Saul's death. He had trusted that if God had truly called him, He would make a way for him to become king.

Does anyone in your life make it hard for you to serve God with a joyous heart? Do you sometimes feel like people don't want you to get to the place God has called you to? Don't worry. That's how David felt too, and look how he responded. Would you respond the same way? Or would you rather rejoice that your enemy had finally died? I hope your response would be the same as David's, because that's God's way.

David's humility always amazes me. He could have shouted in the streets, "I am the anointed of God. Crown me king." But he didn't. He patiently waited for God to place the crown on his head. He wasn't seeking a title. He wanted to honour God!

> *Then it came about afterwards that David inquired of the Lord, saying, "Shall I go up to one of the cities of Judah?" And the Lord said to him, "Go up." So David said, "Where shall I go up?" And He said, "To Hebron." So David went up there... Then the men of Judah came and there anointed David king over the house of Judah.*
> —2 Samuel 2:1–2, 4

Above all things, David sought God first. Before he stepped into action, he made sure it was God's timing. Too many people try to move in God's calling prematurely and fail. It's so important to learn from David, who waited on God for direction even when he could have tried to take the throne on his own.

By obeying God in every area of his life, David got to the place where God wanted him. He stayed faithful and was raised up in God's timing. At thirty years of age, fifteen to sixteen years after his anointing, he was crowned king. It was well worth the wait, for he was thoroughly prepared for the job.

At first, he was only king over Judah, but God had promised he would be king over the entire nation of Israel. Again, David didn't push and try to make his way; he did things God's way. He allowed God to speak for him. He operated under God's guidance and knew God would promote him in due time.

> *So all the elders of Israel came to the king at Hebron, and King David made a covenant with them before the Lord at Hebron; then they anointed David king over Israel. David was thirty years old when he became king, and he reigned forty years. At Hebron he reigned over Judah seven years and six months, and in Jerusalem he reigned thirty-three years over all Israel and Judah.*
>
> —2 Samuel 5:3–5

Another seven years passed before David saw the complete fulfillment of the promise. It took him approximately twenty-one years to see God's vision for his life fulfilled.

I'm sure David became discouraged many times throughout the process. He had many chances to give up and not trust God, but he chose to believe God.

WAIT FOR GOD'S DIRECTION

chapter eight

There are many examples of people throughout history who've had to pass the test of time before walking into the fullness of God's call. Know that you're definitely not alone. The call God has placed on your life is so great that He doesn't want you to mess it up. If you try to do it before His training process is finished, you will fail. Guaranteed. We have to learn to wait on Him. His timing is always best.

Having looked at Jairus, Abraham, Joseph, and David, we see that all of them came to understand that God's timing is best. We need to glean the principles of waiting from their stories. It will help us trust God's timing in our own situations.

Even Jesus had to wait for God's timing before He performed any miracles. Don't you think Jesus saw sick people before he turned thirty? He must have passed by many lame and blind people before He could do anything. He knew His calling. He was sure of why He was there, yet He submitted completely to the Father's will.

The thought that even Jesus needed preparation and had to stand the test of time should speak volumes to us. When God first gives us a vision, why do we think it will be completed in less than a year? We need to be patient.

Trusting God's Timing

Let's take this even further. Think about God Almighty, the maker of heaven and earth. God took thousands of years to fulfill His ultimate plan of salvation through Jesus. God had this plan since the fall of mankind, yet He waited for the perfect timing. What a lesson this is for us.

God wants to send Jesus to us again for a second time. How long has He waited?

> *The Lord is not slow about His promise [of Jesus' return], as some count slowness, but is patient toward you, not wishing for any to perish but for all to come to repentance.*
>
> —2 Peter 3:9

God, too, is patiently waiting for us to do our job. He wants us to bring others into the Kingdom. The problem is, we often deviate from God's plans. We become frustrated and quit too easily.

Always wait for God's direction before taking the next step. We can learn from Moses. While he was leading the people into the wilderness, He always waited on God to see what to do next. He constantly listened for God's guidance.

> *Now the Lord spoke to Moses, saying, "Tell the sons of Israel to turn back and camp before Pi-hahiroth, between Migdol and the sea; you shall camp in front of Baal-zephon, opposite it, by the sea. For Pharaoh will say of the sons of Israel, 'They are wandering aimlessly in the land; the wilderness has shut them in.' Thus I will harden Pharaoh's heart, and he will chase after them; and I will be honored through Pharaoh and all his army, and the Egyptians will know that I am the Lord." And they did so.*
>
> —Exodus 14:1–4

Wait for God's Direction

They had just escaped the Egyptians and plundered them in a miraculous way, but then God seemed to lead them into a dead end. When He told them to camp beside the Red Sea, He was basically sending them into a trap. When Pharaoh came with his army, the Israelites seemingly had nowhere to go.

God's direction for our lives doesn't always make sense right away. It may even look absurd, but God always has the bigger picture in mind. He knows His next step, even if He doesn't reveal it to us. He isn't planning what to do next; He's already planned it. That's why we need to listen to His direction. This is how we'll reach our destiny.

Then the Egyptians chased after them with all the horses and chariots of Pharaoh, his horsemen and his army, and they overtook them camping by the sea, beside Pi-hahiroth, in front of Baal-zephon.
—Exodus 14:9

The Israelites were terrified, as would we be. They had no place to turn but God. He was the only one who could save them. If God had told them to camp there, He must have had a way out. He wouldn't have planned their miraculous victory in Egypt if He didn't plan to deliver them completely. In these situations, we desperately need to turn to God. He's the only one who can do something to change our circumstances.

Since it looked like they were sure to die, the Israelites blamed Moses for leading them there and thought it would have been better if they had died in Egypt (Exodus 14:10–12). Moses heard their accusations against him and began to do what any good faith leader would do. He spoke words of faith to strengthen them. He began with very bold statements.

Trusting God's Timing

But Moses said to the people, "Do not fear! Stand by and see the salvation of the Lord which He will accomplish for you today; for the Egyptians whom you have seen today, you will never see them again forever. The Lord will fight for you while you keep silent."

—Exodus 14:13–14

Moses was a man of faith and boldness. He told the people not to fear, even though in the natural they had every reason to fear. Moses reminded them that God was on their side. God was going to fight for them.

Something very interesting happened next. I think part of the story may not have been recorded. Moses spoke words of faith, and then I believe he cried out to God to truly help them.

Then the Lord said to Moses, "Why are you crying out to Me? Tell the sons of Israel to go forward.

—Exodus 14:15

Leaders often speak words of faith because they know they're true, but these leaders don't know what God's going to do next or what their part is. It's a leader's job to hear God's voice and discover His next step. Moses' exhortation to not fear was very encouraging, but it appears that maybe Moses needed some encouragement as well. I love God's response to this heartfelt cry:

As for you, lift up your staff and stretch out your hand over the sea and divide it, and the sons of Israel shall go through the midst of the sea on dry land. As for Me, behold, I will harden the hearts of the Egyptians so that they will go in after them; and I will be honored through Pharaoh and all his army, through his chariots and his horsemen. Then the

Wait for God's Direction

Egyptians will know that I am the Lord, when I am honored through Pharaoh, through his chariots and his horsemen.
—Exodus 14:16–18

In other words, God said, "Don't just stand there crying—go forward!" Remember, in the natural this was impossible. They had the Red Sea in front of them and the chariots of Pharaoh behind. What God told them to do seemed absurd. It didn't make any sense, but Moses knew this was God's direction. Even though it looked impossible, he had to speak it out to the people.

Notice God's instructions to the Israelites—they were to go forward. And God told Moses that his part was to lift up his staff and stretch out his hand over the sea. Then God would cause the sea to part until the Egyptian army tried to cross over. God gave each one their assignment and also revealed what He was about to do. Always listen to God's directions carefully. Find out what it is you are supposed to do and what He will do.

Then Moses stretched out his hand over the sea; and the Lord swept the sea back by a strong east wind all night and turned the sea into dry land, so the waters were divided. The sons of Israel went through the midst of the sea on the dry land, and the waters were like a wall to them on their right hand and on their left.
—Exodus 14:21–22

Once Moses and the children of Israel were obedient in doing their part, God did His. It was important for them to take the first step of obedience. If they had disobeyed, they would have been killed and not fulfilled God's purposes. God fulfills everything He says He is going to do. He wiped out

Trusting God's Timing

the Egyptian army (Exodus 14:23–31). His power was proven to everyone.

God is calling us to be a people of radical obedience. People who wait on God to hear His directions not only hear them but also obey them, even when they seem contrary to all logic.

These aren't the only times Moses waited for specific direction. Moses waited to hear God speak so many other times in Scripture. What is God speaking to you today? Will you hear His voice? Will you be obedient to everything He tells you to do, even if it doesn't fit your understanding?

In one instance, the Israelites weren't able to find water. Once they finally did, the water was very bitter and no one wanted to drink it. Moses cried out to the Lord and He showed him what to do (Exodus 15:22–25). God will be faithful to guide and direct us. All we have to do is listen and be obedient.

When the people were without food, they began grumbling and complaining. Once again, God told them what He was about to do and what they would have to do to receive His provision (Exodus 16:1–5). God's always willing to tell us His plans, if we will listen.

When things didn't go as planned, Moses sought God's face. He listened for God's voice and allowed Him to speak direction into his life. At most every step, he asked God what to do next and God always responded.

Let this be an example to you. Wait and listen for God's direction. Don't run ahead of Him. Allow Him to fill you in on all His plans. This is the best way for us to follow God and reach our God-given destiny. Even when we appear to be trapped beside the Red Sea, with no way of escape, we can rest assured that God already has the escape route planned. Make it a habit to seek God's face daily. He'll be your best friend and prepare you for what's to come.

CONCLUSION

While on the journey to seeing our promises fulfilled, I believe we need to be thankful, no matter what the situation looks like. I had to relearn this lesson on a recent trip to Honduras where Karla and I ministered with our team to the Tolupan Indians.

We were told ahead of time that this trip wasn't for the weak of heart. It was going to be a tough journey up dirt mountain roads, giving up all comforts in order to preach Jesus to this tribe. We drove for hours up the mountain, taking dangerous curves and crossing rivers where the water came up to the bumper.

The ride there was only the beginning. When we arrived, we realized that we had no telephone or internet signal and were cut off from all communication with normal civilization. Not only that, we had to take freezing cold showers and sleep on a concrete floor in a big room with twenty other people, some who snored loudly. (Some say I snored as well, but I didn't hear it.) There were bugs everywhere and dogs full of fleas came in and out during the day, leaving their fleas behind.

We knew that things would be uncomfortable, but we wanted to bring the love of Jesus to these people who may have never heard it. We were willing to crucify our flesh and allow Christ to shine through us.

On the morning after our first rough night, I was asked to lead worship. I was grateful to do so. As I began to lead the team in singing, I felt the Lord impress on my heart to thank Him for everything we had gone through the night before. We had a powerful time in God's presence as we thanked Him for the bugs, loss of sleep, snoring in harmony, and concrete floors. We had a major breakthrough from that point forward.

As we were singing, I had each member of our team shout out something they had found difficult and then we helped them turn it into praise. As we did this, I was reminded of a very important scripture:

> *Therefore by Him let us continually offer the sacrifice of praise to God, that is, the fruit of our lips, giving thanks to His name.*
>
> —Hebrews 13:15

It was amazing when we sensed the power of God hitting the place. We all began to praise Jesus like never before. A fresh sense of thankfulness came into our hearts, preparing us for the ministry that was to come. Over the next few days, we saw people saved, healed, and delivered.

I realized that we need to thank God at all times, even when there's no comfort or communication and tough circumstances surround us. We're not supposed to praise Jesus only when things are going well for us. It's awesome to praise Jesus when it's a sacrifice to do so. It would have been easy to complain the whole trip and probably not accomplish anything, but instead we gave shouts of sacrificial praise unto Jesus. Through this, each team member was encouraged and God broke through with His love, not only for the Tolupan Indians but also for us.

Conclusion

The Bible also tells us, *"Rejoice always; pray without ceasing; in everything give thanks; for this is the will of God for you in Christ Jesus"* (1 Thessalonians 5:16–18).

Notice that Paul doesn't tell us to just give thanks when all is going well. He says that we should give thanks in everything. Whether or not things seem to be going well for us, we must not lose focus. The best thing to do is praise Jesus, because He knows what's best for us. There's a reason we go through the things we do. God has a good plan despite the current circumstances.

As we praise Jesus, our focus shifts to Jesus and off our circumstances. Jesus gets exalted in our lives, which brings joy to God's heart. Our struggles lessen as we learn to give Him thanks in everything, good or bad.

So wherever you are in your journey to seeing God's promise fulfilled in your life, give Him praise. Lift up His name today and thank Him even for the hard things you don't understand just yet. As you do, He'll breathe fresh hope into your life.

Take a moment as you put down this book to thank Jesus for everything He's done for you. Tell Him that you believe the promise He gave you and knows that He's able and willing to fulfil it. Just raise your hands and give Him thanks.

Once God has placed His vision in your heart, you can be sure He will fulfill it. Continue to serve God where you are and know He'll promote you when He sees fit. Just continue to love on Him and serve Him with your whole heart.

Don't get discouraged when things get tough. Remind yourself of what others had to go through before they saw the fullness of their vision. When you hit the bumpy road where nothing seems to go right or nothing is happening at all, know that God is fighting for you. When you want to give up, trust that God's going to give you strength as you wait on Him.

Trusting God's Timing

Do you not know? Have you not heard? The Everlasting God, the Lord, the Creator of the ends of the earth does not become weary or tired. His understanding is inscrutable. He gives strength to the weary, and to him who lacks might He increases power. Though youths grow weary and tired, and vigorous young men stumble badly, Yet those who wait for the Lord will gain new strength; they will mount up with wings like eagles, they will run and not get tired, they will walk and not become weary.

—Isaiah 40:28–31

Your victory is about to come. The call of God is on your life and you're going to fulfill it as you submit to His will. Your life will shine with Jesus's love to the world.